Home Workshop
Professional
Lock Tools

by eddie the wire

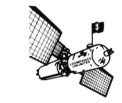

Loompanics Unlimited
Port Townsend, Washington

Home Workshop Professional Lock Tools

Published by:
Loompanics Unlimited
PO Box 1197
Port Townsend, WA 98368
Loompanics Unlimited is a division of Loompanics Enterprises, Inc.

Cover design and illustrations by Kevin Martin

ISBN 1-55950-136-7
Library of Congress Card Catalog 95-81195

Contents

Cautions, Rejoinders, and Disclaimers:

The least serious charge involved in any burglary is breaking and entering, but it is a two-part thing. You can break a lock *or* any other part of a house or grounds, or you can enter any part of the house or grounds. The entering part can be as trivial as the mere insertion of a probe into a lock, or putting the tip of a fishing pole through an open window. The law is specifically left very loose for ease of prosecution, so all burglars aspiring to a greater level of skill than the Watergators displayed, heed well this warning.

Loompanics, and/or eddie the wire, assume no responsibility whatsoever for any damages incurred, either real or incidental, as a result of the proper use or misuse of the information contained herein.

The making, use, or possession of the tools and appliances described herein may be illegal in some jurisdictions, and Loompanics, and/or eddie the wire, assume no responsibility whatsoever for any damages incurred, either real or incidental, as a result of the manufacture of these tools.

Please be sure to observe all manufacturers' safety precautions when using any of the tooling, materials, and techniques described herein.

Dedication

Here's the real story. Eddie's dad supplemented his scant post-war income by performing, doing short skits and playing music (his real love) for a short period, and his act needed specialty equipment which led him to a magicians' supplier. Eddie's dad later took him to this truly wonderful place and bought him a book on escape-artist techniques that was to be the start of eddie's education into the mysteries of lock picking. In it were the first pick profiles eddie ever saw, and ever applied to those first three padlocks without keys. After a short illness, eddie's dad passed away last year, and this book is in love dedicated to him and to the mom who always needed her kitchen outlet "fixed," and to 3 Louis who knows who he is.

Chapter One
Foreword

Anybody who's been to a locksmiths' conference or even a local meeting knows that the real lowdown you get comes at the bar after the meeting while talking with other locksmiths. Starting from a friendly swap of oddball key codes and sneaky tricks, invariably these sessions produce a "I know something hot that you don't" discussion and it was at one of these that I displayed one of my first bench-made picks. That is really how this whole thing started. A few of the guys wanted to know where to buy one of those ultra-skinny picks, and I just had to mouth off and explain that I had made it myself. That started a flood of questions that eventually seems to have led to *PLT (How to Make Your Own Professional Lock Tools, Volume One)* being written. After three more PLT books and a long time lapse, eddie the wire now offers you this book. It is a complete update of *PLT 1-4* with nearly double the material and new and better ways of doing almost everything in the way of making lock picks.

How frustrating would it be if you could magically learn everything a master locksmith knew about picking locks, but didn't have the actual tools used to pick a lock? Now reverse that problem. Suppose you bought an entire tool case from a master locksmith, but had no idea how to use the myriads of tools inside. The point is that both the book-learning of lock picking techniques and the workshop making of the tools to pick locks are two halves of the same skill.

Any professional locksmith who has not learned the art of making tools and made a personal set is missing the boat. You will not get the best use of your skill from using an off-the-shelf trade set. Similarly, the pickmaker also must be skilled in locksmith picking abilities in order to know what design and qualities to shoot for in tools. Of course you must also know exactly how or why the tools and techniques work.

While there are at least a few books in print (and not restricted) on lock picking skills, there is little or nothing on making tools. This book will lead you step-by-step in the hand crafting of lock picks. Master the skills revealed in this book and your picks will be the finest available. You will be able to make dozens of pick designs that do not even exist on the commercial market. The CIA should be so lucky as to have this book on file.

When I started my apprenticeship as a locksmith, I remember well the day I was first initiated into the mysteries of the lock pick. My teacher opened his hip wallet (the big kind with the leather fold-out side wings) to reveal at least fifty types of picks. I asked him which type went to what lock and he did something I will never forget. He reached in and pulled out a single lifter lock pick, and said "This is the only style you ever need use." After a year I realized he was both right and wrong. The commercial pick assortments have lots of rake-style picks but only one or two types of lifter. What he said that was right is that only a lifter-type attack guarantees an opening (if you do it right). What was wrong was that many more than two or three lifters are needed. The master locksmith finds that no less that seven or eight different lifters are a working minimum tool kit.

At some point early on in any aspiring locksmith's practice, although possessing a fair amount of skill at the pure techniques of lock picking, he just plain cannot open this or that lock no matter what. Did the skill level go down, was the lock defective or jammed up slightly... what's the story? The smith who really wants to know might take a lock of that same make and model and examine it on the bench, working it over to find out what makes it different from the rest, if anything. The real answer lies in a little-known truth. The locks are not so much to blame, nor are the skills; the tools are the real problem. Locksmiths deal every day with an increasingly vast number of different lock brands and/or code series, each one designed to a specific set of keyway dimensions and bitting increments. Code books and key blanks to service each lockset that may walk in the shop or appear in the field are the essential tools of the trade, and incidentally that's what separates the pro from the key cutters.

With all this vast library of variations in cuts, depths, angles, increments, and warding variations it is naive to assume that a working set of three lifter lock picks will fit every lock. The best chance of success when doing a pure picking opening is the utilization of a correspondingly large number of opening tools that are matched to each lock! It has been my experience that such tools, custom-designed for a given keyway and set of bitting increments, will greatly increase the ease of any such opening. A side benefit is in technique, which seems to improve when the working feeling of a tool is the same for vastly different locks, because the tool puts consistency into the envelope of manipulation.

Since no such set of tooling lists from any supply house, the first step along these lines is in filing down the shank on a commercial pick to get more clearance in some keyway. We've all done this at some time, often with a bit of "I'll get you" desperation at some balky lock. You soon find out that the shank can stand only a little thinning before it caves in. The problem is usually an indifferently tempered low carbon steel. Altering the tip working height is another common step. It is easy to file it lower, but so difficult to file it higher. After a few trials trying such more or less random alterations, you will either give up or you may ask around for some master-level knowledge. The purpose of this book is to give you those skills.

In other words, the master locksmith can only do the best job using tools that cannot be purchased, but instead must be made. This book will tell you how to design and make those lock picks in the easiest, best ways possible.

You will learn that a lock pick is a tool at its best because it must excel at being as strong as possible, yet be as small as possible. Only attention to detail and care will produce such a minimal tool. Commercially available picks fall way short on accuracy and cross section. They have actually very large profiles to compensate for the poor strength that low-carbon steel offers, and to minimize the warpage a small shank will undergo due to the punching process. A better steel would allow that smaller working cross-section, but is difficult to punch cleanly without heavy punch die wear and high costs. Because the steel in commercial picks is of low quality, grinding the shank to more acceptable working dimensions at your own shop only causes you grief when that pick bends from lack of strength.

The advantage for hand-finished tools then is their minimal, unique designs executed in high strength carbon steel. The uniqueness of picks that you have designed and built for yourself is easily worth the effort of mastering the skills of making them.

There are other advantages in taking time to learn how to produce your own personal tool systems for lock picking. You can design and build a lock pick and promptly get ideas on its performance by using it in day-to-day field servicing. By doing this your designs will evolve and mature and in turn your hand technique will modify and improve to match your tools. Some of the pick designs I commonly rely on and produce today have undergone five or six cycles of modification. One of my friends might come in and complain he couldn't get this so-and-so pick into such-and-such a lock, so I measured it and cut it to another likely size. A week later he came back all smiles and I made a note of the lock type and the new size.

Anything you can imagine can be designed and built. Those first tools will be followed by gradually refined designs. Eventually the layout of a set of picks will be based completely on working drawings with nothing left to chance, and it is then that your pick-making skills must really be up to speed.

Once designs are completed the primary concern in lock pick making becomes precision execution. It is very easy to grind right up to the layout lines and finish the pick with a #4 die file, but you cannot really know what the actual dimensions of the pick tip are until you gauge them with the proper instruments. As little as eight-thousandths of an inch either way will noticeably affect pick feel, so you should make and use a set of working drawings, and learn to follow them. No extensive precision tooling is required to gauge work with tolerances in the + or − .008 range, just a dial caliper, a tool all locksmiths should possess anyway. A rough record of each design's use, lock preferences, and reliability is maintained, and filed with the working drawing for that pick, so that it can be altered if improvements suggest themselves. This dictates that your work is precise at the beginning so you can modify the pick design with the same tolerance as it was built to. If records are not kept, an unusually good working design will be hard to duplicate. Measuring with great precision also makes it easier to finish a pick. Instead of guessing, you will KNOW if it's right.

One other thing needs pointing out. After the fourth or fifth keyway you tool up for, you may have twenty or more tools, each almost identical to the others to the naked eye. The temptation is strong then to settle for these twenty. My advice is don't do it. Knowing that you are using a pick sized to match a keyway gives you a good psychological boost during an opening attempt, and as your experience with custom tools grows, it becomes self-evident to you that those size variations of five- or ten-thousandths will indeed spell the difference between an easy working and failure. Develop as large a working base of tools as you can, and keep them all in good working condition. The time saved will more than compensate for the effort. Before we start cutting steel allow eddie a brief moment of philosophizing, if you please.

Have you ever wondered just exactly why lock picking is viewed with such fascination by people in all walks of life? I get mail from all over the map and I often wonder about the almost universal attraction. Doctors, teachers, whoever; show them a lock pick set and the interest level soars. The desire to learn the art of picking a lock has complex roots. To some it is puzzle-solving on a mechanical hands-on level, kind of like a high-tech wire nail puzzle. Charles Babbage, the inventor of the mechanical computer, was reportedly very interested in locks and their picking.

For others it is the satisfaction of being immune to being locked out of anything no matter what the lock is, to have the necessary skill to wield that magic passkey where others cannot. To many it is belonging to a small and secretive group of people who know how to pick a lock, like secret agents, detectives and skilled gem thieves. Merely being in the know when someone else discourses on the subject of lock picking, and knowing the jargon for lock picking like "plug wrench," "ball pick" and so on is exciting to many. With eddie it was the same, at first. I wanted to be able to pick, pick quickly, and pick well, just like in the movies. After that wore off I still wanted to pick, but to pick and rarely, if ever, to be defeated by a lock. Nothing can match the frustration level of a guy who uses a lock pick on a lock and ends up on the outside looking in. It's worse than dealing with the government! Eddie's resolve to make his openings quicker and cleaner led to making tools that would actually work. Nearly twenty years later, eddie's tools are even better.

As a parting comment, because of the mind set of the lock pick artists they are often drawn to other fields. In particular master lock pick experts often enjoy learning playing-card manipulations like second dealing, the pass, the side slip, and so on. Not self-working card tricks, but pure skill moves. I'm proud of this new book series, and I think it will be the bible on the subject for a generation or so. In the interest of making it the absolute complete guide, I have compiled a list of some great card manipulation books. Most are in print, most are really reasonable. Try reading and doing tricks and whatever from this list. It may not increase your lock picking skill physically, but it may put you more in the mindset.

Card Control: Practical Methods & Forty Original Card Experiments, by Arthur H. Buckley, Dover, 1993.

The Card Magic of Le Paul, published by EZ Magic/D. Robbins Co.

Roughingly Yours, by Aldini. Mickey Hades Enterprises.

Expert Card Technique, by Jean Hugard and Frederick Braue. Dover, 1975.

Card Manipulations, by Jean Hugard. Dover, 1993.

Greater Magic: A Practical Treatise on Modern Magic, by John N. Hilliard. Visionary Experiences, 1994.

Chapter Two
Lock Pick Design Principles

Understanding how a lock pick acts on the lock mechanism makes it easier to make good lock pick design decisions. So before attempting to learn lock pick design principles, you should first have a working knowledge of the operation of each of the four main lock types; in order of complexity they are: 1) warded locks; 2) disc tumblers; 3) pin tumblers; and 4) lever tumblers. You must fully understand how each part works in relation to the other parts, and mentally you must be able to project how each part of the system interacts. Trouble is, this book would be twice as large if I explained all that, so I'll concentrate on making tools. *The Complete Guide to Lock Picking* covers skills and the "eddie" way.

Lock pick design decisions have just one goal: adjusting the range of motion or action of the part of the pick that enters the keyway. The goal is to apply pressure exactly where it is needed while avoiding tool contact with parts in the lock you wish to leave undisturbed. "Range of motion" might be better expressed as "envelope," an area within which the pick can work safely.

These two design limitations of the lock pick dictate opposite goals, namely that the pick be as strong as necessary, yet be as small as possible. Simply put: the more working slack in the keyway, the easier to work the lock, but a too-small tool will fold under lifting pressure.

The "parts you want to avoid" are of course all the tumblers you are not trying to presently lift or manipulate. The "Friday the 13th" type opening is when you are working a back tumbler that must be picked first because it is binding first, and a front tumbler that has a very low combination (a deep key cut). This means any fat shank problems will lift, perhaps overlift the deep key cut tumbler, and if it

gets overlifted and hangs up above the shear line, man, you got troubles many. That's why this chapter is here. Just worried about fat shanks? Suppose the range of motion of your lifter is insufficient to lift that back tumbler fully without the shank angling up enough to bump again on that front tumbler? That's a problem that is specific not so much to the particular lock type as to the key or the tumbler coding. The lock pick artist expresses it as a tumbler code because keys are never worried about things like first binding tumblers.

Working with the design process will also add to your physical picking skill in an ongoing way. If you have verified that your design will move and act in a certain way inside the lock, then you have a mental goal that can be transferred into positive "feel" feedback when working the lock. You have a target to work for.

Let's begin the design process by drawing up a list of requirements. We need some hard performance numbers to start with.

The first consideration is the thickness of the pick stock that should be selected. This is the only dimension that is difficult to alter quickly by grinding, although you will learn how to wedge or sharpen the very tip of a lifter to get it to "dig in" to a tumbler surface. A lock pick could be as thick as the keyway across were it not for the warding of the keyway. Warding and mushroom tumblers are the two major anti-pick systems employed.

Remember that the highest warding projecting into the keyway is what the lower tumblers bottom out or rest on! To do this job the warding must project to almost the middle of the tumblers. Some types of locks have warding that extends well past the midline of the tumblers, and furthermore in some other makes of lock the warding is very thick (up to down). Both of these types of warding limit very free access of the pick tip to the tumbler ends. That's the whole idea.

It should be noted that then higher-security locks, like early-style Yales, incorporated both types of warding into their design. The early Yale lock designer was intent on making their "new" locking system pick proof, so they developed this system which is called paracentric warding. Naming things by throwing in Greek and Latin root words was fashionable at that time, and indicated high class goods. Paracentric is Latin for beyond or past the center of something. The warding projects past the center of the keyway.

The question we are trying to get around to is how thick to make the lock pick steel. I could just tell you, but I want you to know why. Stick with me and read on.

In modern security design, the cost of production is king. It gets more attention than high-security questions, and since paracentric warding is very costly both in key blanks and other areas of manufacture, today's keyways are much less restrictive. Since the 1920s, the U.S. Government Postal Service has purchased the copyrights to several of the Yale keyways for exclusive Postal use. This move was done mostly to limit the commercial availability of key blanks which would obviously compromise the security of the Postal system. If you have your own keyway, you have the highest security from most key duplication. Since most of these keyway profiles were of the difficult paracentric design, it is wise to have tools that will defeat these as well. I made a conscious decision to design those of my tools that were not targeted for a specific brand or keyway so that they would function in the difficult paracentric warding

geometry. This means they enjoy just that much more warding clearance when working the average lock.

Examine Figure 1 and you will notice how two different warding systems work to limit pick access. This relationship is the most important factor to consider when selecting a pick thickness. In locks like the "Best" brand, the keyway is severely choked by the warding and the lifter pick designed for this lock must be higher than the average to span the diagonal, yet still very thin to fit in the space available. The warding that projects into the cylinder key slot is designed to limit access and elbow room in this critical area. The corrugation or profile of the key blank is radically offset to clear this warding and so the smaller the tool thickness the more room in the area defined by the end of the warding and the side of the keyway.

After long experience I have come up with the following rule of thumb for thickness selection, and another rule for width of pick shank. Notice that a thicker steel can use a thinner width and vice versa.

Thicknesses in the .025 to .031″ range seem to be the most practical balance between strength and thinness, and a shank width of .045-.050″ with a thickness of .025-.031″ is my usual starting point in design. Let me emphasize that I have made picks as light as .020″ thick also. The relationship between thickness and shank width is a ratio. A thinner pick has to have a wider shank and so on. It is not a one-to-one ratio. If bending is a problem with a .050″ width shank pick, thickness must be increased far more to compensate for this, so the .031″ is home base, so to speak. Not by chance it is also the thickest dimension you can easily obtain shim stock in. Not only do thickness and width combine to set the total

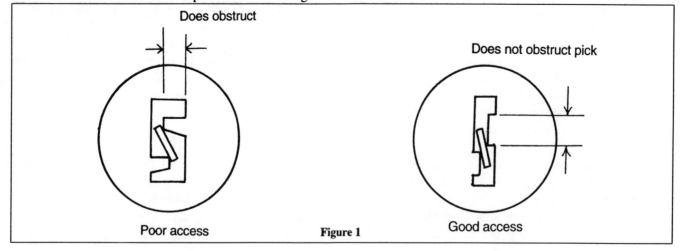

Does obstruct

Poor access

Does not obstruct pick

Good access

Figure 1

bending resistance, you must also consider the amount of force that needs to be applied. Suppose you had a really strong pick, say .031″ thick and .075″ shank width. Such a tool could easily move a weight like a shot glass full of J.D. across a table without hardly flexing. To verify this make sure to try it at least four different times by emptying and refilling the shot glass. This is called the empirical scientific method. Now try to move an eight ounce tumbler of J.D. and that strong pick flexes way over and probably takes a permanent set or bend. The difference is the amount of force that must be applied. The questions are: how much pressure is needed to lift up a pin tumbler; how strong is that spring; and how much drag is caused by the friction of the pin sliding in the lock as you apply turning pressure to the core with the tension wrench? You can take it from me that the spring tension is usually very slight. Most locks are provided with springs that are easily flexed with the very weakest of pick shanks. So it's reduced to a three-way split of pick shank strength, amount of turning tension applied (operator) and the ability of the tension wrench itself to transmit turning force without bending as well.

Beginning lock pick artists are continually reminded not to apply too much wrench tension to the lock for that very reason. Excessive twist will make even the strongest pick bend.

So let's leave the lock pick briefly and examine some tension wrench criteria. As you know, the whole object of picking an individual tumbler, either a pin or a disc tumbler, is to lift it with a tool until its edge catches and holds on the shoulder or lip created by the misalignment of the cylinder and the keyway plug. As eddie says, it is easy to build a torque wrench tool that can exert so much force on the sides of the tumbler via the plug that the pick will bend instead of overcoming the friction and lifting the tumbler. Should you then make the torque wrench weaker, or use it with a weaker hand, exerting less force so the pick will not bend? Do you make the pick stronger to compensate? Consider the system mentally or on scratch paper before you answer these questions. Try to simulate various tool design approaches and see them in your mind's eye before you try them.

The essential question to ask is: "How little turning torque will hold the tumblers up at the shear line without their springs slipping them back off?"

You may be surprised at the negligible amount of weight necessary to hold a pin tumbler, and therefore the tiny amount of additional friction bearing on the pin tumbler over and above the usual spring tension of the tumbler driver spring. With such a small amount of friction to overcome, the lock pick can have a correspondingly very small cross-section without bending in the lock. We never did answer the question asked in the first paragraph; is it better to make the tension wrench weak so as not to "freeze" the pins with excessive torque, or make the pick stronger? The answer is to make the pick as small (and therefore weak) as possible, and allow excessive tension or torque to be controlled firstly by the operator, secondly by the springiness of the tool shank, and I'll explain this in detail. The itty-bitty living room of the keyway usually leaves picks cut to fit comfortably within it pretty weak, so strong picks are usually not a big problem.

There are two types of wrench "feel" to experiment with, and two types of tip fit. Those wrenches with rigid, heavy shanks often also have the tight fitting tips, and those wrenches with light springy shanks have the loose fitting tips. But, it is by no means written in stone that you cannot build a springy shanked wrench with a tight fitting tip, or vice versa. This freedom of design is what makes the locksmith who builds his own tools the one who succeeds in opening locks more times than his unskilled counterpart. Picking styles will again vary widely, but you should know the advantages of each type, as it will aid you in pick designing. The squishy feel of a lightweight shank can rob you of tumbler feedback. Tumbler feedback is when you feel the pin throughout its entire movement up to the shear line. This feedback allows you to adjust wrench tension precisely, and detect if a pin is being lifted beyond the shear line.

A solid shank, however, still demands a springy grip (not necessarily a loose grip) to produce that vital lightness of torsion. Put another way, it is much easier to over-torsion a lock cylinder with a solid shanked tension wrench than it is with a springy shanked wrench. It is perhaps this fact that makes the springy shank more of a pop culture favorite, since it requires less initial skill in manipulation, and one size fits many. Superior picking technique also demands that the wrench tension must vary during the opening. This wrench manipulation is at least as important as the pick movement itself, and the two always complement each other.

To provide the best possible feel if you are just starting out as a locksmith, try a tricky bit of tool design. The wrench is cut from wire stock whose shank has been ground very slim over a long portion of its shank for the springy feel, but the tip is left very tight in its fit to the keyway under attack. It is that tight, almost wedging fit that ensures good feedback while still retaining the advantage of a springy shank. The springy wrench will always allow finer increments of tension with less muscle tension in the hands. In very tight-fitted locks the loose fit tip, such as comes from cutting out of shim stock instead of wire, will slip and slide under the very low torque required, often fumbling away from the lock and making repicking necessary.

The amount of torque a given wrench exerts also depends on how long it is and where the fingers will contact it to manipulate. The almost universal practice for the key-in-knob lock is to hold onto the doorknob with the left hand fingers and manipulate the wrench with the thumb. This practically limits the working length of the wrench to about three inches. In most other situations, such as pin tumbler cylinders set flush with door surfaces, the hand manipulated tension wrench is still most comfortable at this same length, and I have standardized on this length by producing 6″ wrenches with two working ends. Many operators sneak a finger or two around the slight protrusion of the cylinder to anchor their hand for precise manipulation. I also do this. The effective working length thus remains three inches or so due to finger/thumb length.

I would like to point out that once the pick shank has been slimmed to its desired width overall, it is still possible to do spot slimming right at the radius tip of the tool, especially in a lifter. The actual tip may also be reduced to a near-knife edge by filing on the SIDES of the pick tip. This results in no real loss of strength, since the force is exerted almost straight up and down and the pick will have enormous strength in that position. This near-knife edge seems to offer a better feel in determining which tumbler is which, and the keen edge will also bite into the brass and keep the tool tip from sliding off the polished tumbler surface into areas where its intrusion may be undesirable. It is also possible to slim the thickness of the pick back into the shank area, but the temptation to do this should be avoided; in short, don't do it.

There is a tendency when cutting or slimming a pick either in width or thickness to cut off just one more little shaving. The psychology of the cutting process is that less steel will give you a better chance at using the pick successfully, so the brain thinks more cutting is better, but the more time expended in cutting the more you will lose if you make a tool that crumples when first used. Avoid over slimming, over cutting, and never cut down the shank width past a proven smallest width. Never ever alter shank thickness from what the shim stock was packaged as. You will lose far more than you will gain, since side-to-side clearance past the wards is usually not a critical problem, nearly as much as up-and-down clearance past the tumblers.

It is a very good idea for you to start a library or card file listing information that you will accumulate over your career. The form I use is reproduced on page 9, and you have permission to reproduce it as well for your own private files. I got this idea when I did some work for a precinct house and had to walk through the latent print classification office several times to get to the cages. Their cards looked like a pretty good layout and so I copied one and came up with a system of my own. Notice that it lists tip angle (both lead and rebate) shank length, shank width and taper, pull angle, tip height, bias (if any), thickness, and handle details. This card has a cross reference number on it that keys to another card file of keyways.

A final word: the lock pick artist who can't master a lock will never know why unless he examines the tool design to prove that it is physically capable of doing that lock. Just cussing out the lock or the pick won't get you in, or make your skills better. By contrast, whoever opens a lock has two sources of pride: not only did you do the impossible and pop the lock, you actually made the tool that made the opening possible. Nothing compares to that lift.

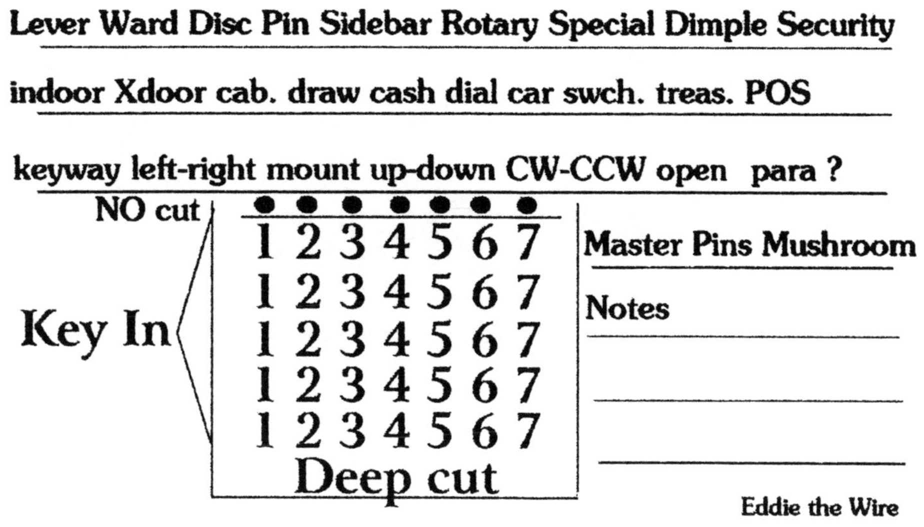

Lever Ward Disc Pin Sidebar Rotary Special Dimple Security

indoor Xdoor cab. draw cash dial car swch. treas. POS

keyway left-right mount up-down CW-CCW open para ?

NO cut

● ● ● ● ● ● ●

Key In

1 2 3 4 5 6 7   **Master Pins Mushroom**
1 2 3 4 5 6 7   **Notes**
1 2 3 4 5 6 7
1 2 3 4 5 6 7
1 2 3 4 5 6 7
Deep cut

Eddie the Wire

Figure 2
Lock Classifying Form. Circle each row for lock type, lock mount, keyway details and
circle suspected bitting depth for each tumbler stack and join circles with graph-like lines.

Chapter Three
Steel Stock

The raw material you will be cutting most of your picks from is called feeler gauge or precision ground gauge stock. It comes in different steel alloys like stainless, high- and low-carbon steel, and different hardness tempers from brittle to blue spring. Each type has different characteristics, since it is targeted to a specific kind of industrial shim usage. Eddie considers the spring tempered high-carbon type the best for making lock picks. This is not surprising considering the capacity of high carbon steel for high hardening yet allowing re-tempering to precise specs. The brand I used twenty years back was made by DiArcro Co. but this is difficult to obtain now. A good substitute is Precision brand C1095 steel, and it comes pre-hardened and tempered to Rockwell 48-62. The Rockwell scale is a measure of what degree of temper the steel has been treated to be. It is gauged by pressing a small point into the surface of the steel with a predetermined force, and then measuring the depth to which this force was able to drive the point into the sample being tested. The tempers and Rockwell numbers are listed in the next column, but they are not important to know, just interesting. Don't spend any time memorizing Rockwell tables.

The Precision company also offers a low-carbon product called 1010 steel shim, but this is unusable for picks because it will not hard temper. It is supplied in 6″ and greater widths, and so is not easily confused with the C1095. If in doubt, ask, since the low-carbon will only waste your time. Shim or feeler stock is surface ground to a tolerance of .00067″ plus or minus, and has excellent alloy consistency from batch to batch. It is the only material you should consider for picks. Take advantage of the mighty industrial machine that kicked ass in WWII and buy the best. It's obtainable for just pennies.

HEAT TREATMENT OF METALS
Hardness Conversion Table

Rockwell C 150 kg. Load 120° Diamond	Tensile Strength 1000 psi
--	*440*
--	*420*
--	*401*
70	*384*
68	*368*
66	*352*
64	*337*
62	*324*
60	*311*
58	*298*
57	*287*
55	*276*
53	*266*
52	*256*
50	*247*
49	*238*
47	*229*
46	*220*
45	*212*
44	*204*

Figure 3
Rockwell Numbers

Temper Color of Steel	Degrees F.
Faint yellow	430
Straw color	460
Dark straw	470
Brown yellow	500
Purple	530
Blue	550
Full blue	560
Polish blue	580
Dark blue	600
Pale blue	610

Figure 3a

Hacksaw blades are too uneven in temper, pallet banding too low-carbon; no matter anyway, nothing is as good as shim. It is the perfect product for picks, cheap at the price, and of superior quality. I have never had so much as one bad piece at all. The industrial machine in America can supply you with the best available, so use it with pride. I will say that foreign or imported shim is coming on the market, especially in 50 foot coils. But if you can't get a brand name or find one on the packaging, I would not recommend it. Stick with the domestic stuff.

This same advice applies to using plumbing snake as stock. This steel is or rather used to be suitable, but recent samples are not of sufficient carbon content to make a good pick. Also, eddie's picks have gotten a lot slimmer in width as his technique has improved. If you cut two identical picks, one plumbing snake and one from shim stock, and start slimming the width, the snake will fold early on and the shim won't. At eddie's shop it's called an envelope. The envelope of a given steel or a given pick is its working ability measured by how small a throat it can pass, yet how much force it can exert without bending. See Figure 4. For a superior envelope use only the best.

It is worth noting that shim steel as supplied is tempered a little bit softer than it should be for lock picks with very minimal shanks (extreme envelopes). In the chapter on custom tempering of pick shanks, eddie talks about making that specialized harder pick for a difficult job, like very limited keyway access. For these pick tools, which are cut narrower than normal, a harder temper will work better without fracturing. It is not a hard and fast thing, and you may develop a different preference for degree of hardness

(springiness) as you gain experience using your tools. The difference between custom hardness and temper-as-supplied is very slight for a beginner. It is better that you should use the steel tempered as is until you gain experience, but an expert lock pick operator will always adjust temper to suit.

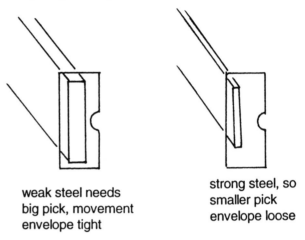

weak steel needs big pick, movement envelope tight

strong steel, so smaller pick envelope loose

Figure 4

Since the legitimate use for shim stock is to shim parts to precise relationships, it necessarily demands a very wide range of sizes. It is usually supplied in .001″ steps up to .025″ and from there in skipping steps to .034″ thick. It is available in 12″ and 5″ flat lengths and 25′ coils. It is tempting to order in the finished 5″ size for grinding integral-handle picks, so go ahead. The coil offers a broader choice of lengths, and since eddie constantly experiments, he uses coil exclusively in the shop. It is quite possible that you may prefer and settle on a working length above or below the usual 5 to 5½″ average. For these lengths a coil stock works better than 5″ or 12″ pieces. A further advantage is if you buy shim stock in the 25-foot coil, those more desirable smaller sizes may still be chopped off from the coil, and without any waste at all. Don't get me wrong on losing a little bit of shim steel. Wasting steel by leaving a lot of ends here and there is not any concern, in the final analysis. The average lifetime steel bill for maintaining a working set of lock picks is so insignificant, it does not pay you to economize with it at all.

The coil is under tension and it can get away from you as you unpack it unless you take precautions. The recommended method is to sandwich it between two pine boards, and put one foot on this sandwich on the floor while you cut the holding bands. Some steel is packaged in self-dispensing cardboard boxes and need not be unpacked further. If you use the foot-long steel, it can be removed and wiped with a rag soaked in lacquer thinner to remove the packing grease, and then laid on top of the sleeve it came in. Ten or twelve of them can be aligned on the workbench and sprayed all at once with layout dye. After a minute of dry time they can all be replaced in their sleeves and held until needed. This will give the dye a chance to age. Layout dye will rub off on your hands if you subject it to hard pressure and water (rough grinding) while still soft, so let it dry a day or so. The dye mark on the sleeve tells you it's ready for layout. That about covers pick steels, so let's look at tension wrench stock.

For making tension wrenches, Precision also offers drill rod and music wire products that work well. The music wire comes in a coil, or it can be specially ordered in cut and straightened lengths, and the sizes run from .006″ to .187″. The steel is a high-carbon alloy. The drill rod is a far better choice for tension wrenches. It comes pre-straightened, and the water hardening W-1 is in the same general alloy family of steels as their feeler stock. Since you will be heating and tempering the tension wrenches considerably, and under bench conditions of less than perfection, the W-1 or the O-1 is far preferable to the more temperamental music wire, which is difficult to consistently control when hardening with a gas torch. The music wire is also available at the hobby shop, and quality is usually good. Even though it's called music wire, it will not be found at a guitar or keyboard shop.

When you have standardized on a pick working length, you can then spend an hour or so and cut the entire buy to size for enough tooling to last for three or four keyway set-ups. For the very fortunate tool-owner the steel may be power-sheared. A year's supply of cutting would only take ten minutes on a machine like a cold shear. If you can locate one in a nearby machine job shop take your steel down and get it processed. As an alternative, the locksmith's grinding wheel can be used. Instead of cutting through the width of the steel, turn it so the shim stock face is at the wheel's outer edge and cut through the thickness of the steel with a corner of the wheel. Stop and softly bend and break it off when the tempering color starts to show through at the middle. If you bend before the steel is very weak, you will curve the ends. These curves must be removed or

straightened, so use only a very little finger pressure to do the break. If the steel resists just grind a little more. The end can then be squared by being coolant-ground to remove the burned steel at the cut ends. Remember that semi-abusing the sharp corner of the wheel like this means you must frequently redress the wheel to restore just the wheel corner.

Chapter Eleven on tension wrenches refers to melting pieces of wire off to form lengths for tension wrenches, and the same technique can be used to melt off lengths of shim stock for picks. If your oxy-acetylene torch will heat the steel fast enough, even a heat sink is unnecessary. Just aim the flame in the middle at the cut line and wait until small sparks spontaneously form. The sparks are an indicator that the steel is heated enough to combust chemically. A second or two later the steel will droop and fall off. As in making tension wrenches, the cut pieces should be arranged to fall in a tray of oil. Eddie prefers olive oil 'cause it smells like cookies baking, but the oil costs like anything. Don't use water because the thermal shock is too great. If the torch heat untempers the steel very far from the melt site, a heat sink may be needed, and a machinist's clamp or locking tweezers will serve well. The real problem with this technique is that it does leave a fairly large band of untempered and curved steel and blobs of steel that must be ground off for the tool to be useful. So while it is easy and quick, it is not very economical. The one advantage is it is so fast. With coils of steel stock you can melt off ten picks just like that, and one end will also be pre-annealed for drilling a hole. For a combination-style tool set, this saves a small step or two. Beware though, because even that small torch can easily draw temper from the entire piece, which would then ruin the working shank. To control the torch burn and anneal precisely, a heat sink is needed.

A set of two small machinist's clamps side-by-side on the shim stock make a desirable heat sink, or even one clamp in a pinch. The steel end area to be cut is inserted between the two, one set back from each projected end with two inches showing. A pair of vise grips applied to the areas where heat is unwanted will also protect the steel. After you fire up the torch keep the heat directly in the middle of the stock, and let the heat build up rapidly in the middle, which will minimize conduction to the ends. Keep the temper a minimum of one and one-half inch from the point where the shank will begin to be ground down.

I should remind you that the bluish or straw oxidation colors blooming on the surface of the steel are proof that the precision factory temper has been shifted softer. These oxidation colors are formed when the exposed surface of the steel goes through a chemical change under heat and parts of the steel alloy combine with the oxygen in air to form compounds that have these colors. Each compound indicates a different temperature level by its color. The physical universe is really well constructed in this regard. The colors can be re-polished back to bright steel when needed to next gauge temperature.

Although grinding is fast, the absolutely quickest way to sever blanks from the steel coil is to fracture the brittle steel with a sharp cold chisel driven by a machinist's hammer. To lay out a cut line, lightly file a line with a triangular single cut, then seat the edge of the chisel into this trough. A strong blow from a sharp chisel cleanly fractures this thin and highly tempered steel like a shot.

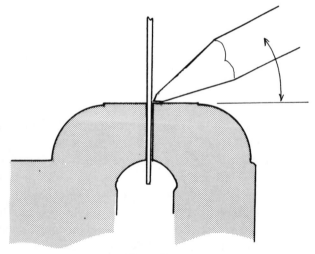

Figure 5
Cutting pick steel blanks with chisel & vise.

It is also possible to clamp the stock in a heavy bench vise with the required length of steel protruding above the jaws of the vise. The cold chisel is applied into the right angle formed by steel and vise jaw top, and the cut made with a sharp rap on the hammer. For a nice cut the chisel should be held at an angle to the face of the steel as in Figure 5. There may be occasional "tearing" of the steel using this method, because the jaws of most bench vises are serrated and will support the stock only intermittently, but these teeth are easily ground flat again during rough shaping. If tearing is not a problem, you may even omit the filed groove.

Methods not to try include any sawing done while the stock is still tempered. It may be done but it's very hard to do. The same also goes for filing through the stock. It is certainly possible, would make a good leisure time or retirement hobby, but is not very practical. If you want to file, grind with the bench wheel instead. Bending and breaking the steel like it was a coat hanger works, but is very time-consuming and the slight curvature it leaves can't be made flat again without a lot of hassle. Stick to the more professional methods of grinding, or cutting with a cold chisel. Abrasive cut-off wheels can be used to make these cuts, but they offer no real advantage over the bench grinding wheel, and generate enough heat to cause tempering problems.

When cutting the steel by shearing action, you may notice that even a partial cut in which the cutting edge of the cold chisel does not extend all the way across the width of the steel, is still sufficient to shear all the way across. This is because the steel has a set of definite crystal fracture lines due to its highly brittle state. It is possible to use this physical fact to advantage and chisel down the length of the stock as well as across it.

Once you have done any pick grinding you will realize that 70% of the production time is spent just grinding one-quarter of the steel blank down to a rough shape. If your workshop is equipped with efficiently built holding jigs, then this time can be passed over automatically. If you sit at the wheel and tend the grinding by hand, a lot of time is wasted. If you observe Figure 6 you will see that a very narrow-faced grinding wheel or jeweler's wheel is used to make the initial depth notch into the steel blank. This notch defines length of working pick shank and also working tip height, since the line starting at its extreme depth will be carried parallel out to the very end of the pick by using the cold chisel. Scoring the steel does seem to produce some definite cut guiding, but the chisel will often have to be moved along the cut and the scoring done pretty heavily. A good pop on the chisel at the first part past the notch sometimes works, sometimes not. It helps to angle the chisel so it cuts right at the notch first. Once the chisel cut to rough width is made, the final grinding is a lot easier. A good operator can become very skilled at using the cold chisel, and may even be able to make the wheel-done starting notch with some light and delicate chisel work instead.

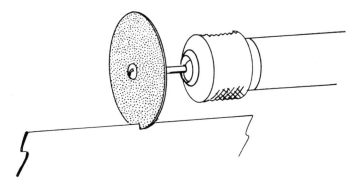

Figure 6
*Cutting initial depth notch in pick stock
with jeweler's wheel.*

Figure 7 shows a mass production jig that can be made to cut shim stock to length and also cut tension wrench stock to length and bend it as well. When cutting shim stock it must be used with coolant spray. The swinging arm labeled B has a steel bushing inserted into the wood. The interior hole of the bushing matches the tension wrench stock diameter. To use the jig a long wire is inserted into the wrench hole and marked at the point it leaves the bushing. Put this wire on a bench and figure out how long you want the wrench handle to be. Make up the rest of the length (marked on the wire) by cutting a filler dowel to size. Now insert the dowel and then insert the wire again and mark it to see if the length is correct. This system allows you to make handles of different lengths just by inserting different length filler dowels. A set of dowels can be marked with pen to indicate the length they create. The dowel is easily removed by tipping the jig upside down.

Once the wrench blank is cut off using the grinding wheel the torch flame is applied to the bend juncture (where it leaves the bushing) and, when cherry red, the arm A is swung over to form the bend. The wrench end is flipped out of the jig, quenched in oil, and the next piece inserted to be cut. It is a mandatory safety ingredient that you have a secure holder for your torch since you will want to keep it lighted during the entire cutting session. It must be picked up and put down safely, so make a good stand. The Smith brand little torch comes with a wire loop that can be screwed into a wooden bench top. Don't attempt to fix the torch in place and swing the jig up

to it. It may save time, but it is way too dangerous to work that close to a live flame.

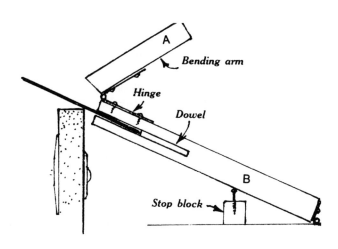

Figure 7
Tension wrench production jig.

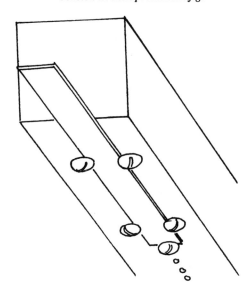

Figure 8
*Tension wrench production jig modification
to cut pick stock to initial length.*

To cut shim stock using the same jig you will need to add a few wood screws in the bottom surface of the B part. Figure 8 shows the pattern of wood screws that will hold the shim stock in place on the B part. Different end screw holes may be drilled to make a variety of lengths. To use, just insert a screw into the desired length hole, and shove in a shim stock under the heads of the wood screws. They can be turned in for a tight shim fit or left as loose as needed, as long as the shim is held safely as it is cut by the grinding wheel. After insertion to the end screw, the A arm is swung down and the shim is cut off. A pointed tool like a screwdriver is needed to unload the cut piece from the embrace of the wood screws. Because of that time element, quenching is unnecessary. Heat from the wheel is not a problem if you use coolant. If you're not set up for coolant yet, just hold a piece of metal against the shim stock and it will act as a heat sink.

Chapter Four
Layout Methods
and Skills

In this chapter, eddie discourses on the perfect methods for putting Ye lines onto Ye steel blank, together with eddie's popular key-part tracing technique for quick and easy pick generation.

Layout is the process of making outlines on steel blanks for grinder cutting by eye, and points for drilling holes. It can be as simple as tracing a part of a key or a master template directly onto a blank, or more complicated, involving geometry and specialized tools. Although layout constructions can be made accurate to + or −.004″ if scribed and executed correctly, the lines are usually used only as rough cutting guides, since the final finishing to shape is done with hand files. The finish filing is guided according to dial vernier measurement or using simple hand methods. The process of layout can be done in two ways.

First of all, a layout can be done by strict measurement. Go one half inch from the edge of your measurement and make another line, then another line a quarter of an inch farther and so on.

Layout can also be unmeasured and still constructive. In other words the layout process itself can produce a line, center, or a set of lines whose position you didn't calculate or measure at all, but which the layout process says are geometrically correct, like the middle of a piece of stock, a right angle line set, and so on. This construction is a function of the properties of right angles, arcs, parallels, and so on, and involves the use of a pair of toolmaker's dividers and a 6″ engraved rule. If you paid attention in your geometry class this is old stuff. If not, it will become real familiar and valuable to you after reading this chapter, and make your geometry professor right when he said you'd be sorry someday if you didn't pay attention.

For straight measure layout the scribers are set using engraved steel rules and dial calipers. Then the measurements are transferred to the blank surface of the dye coated steel pick with dividers and squares.

In order to make the layout lines that you will scribe on the highly polished surface stand out, the steel must be treated with a non-reflective dark chemical coating called layout dye. It comes in either a brush-top can or in a handy spray can, the spray being better for lots of lock pick blanks done at once. Any substitutes like ordinary enamel paint or gun blue will not allow a fine line, and will flake or tear off the steel. Stick to formula layout dye. In addition to the layout dye you need a good scriber. A steel scriber with a very slender point is best for this type of work. A fat prick-awl point is a poor substitute for a machinist's scriber. The usual combination square often has a thin scriber tucked away inside it, with only the knurled brass knob handle showing. In a pinch even a sharp sewing needle works. A carbide tip makes a deep line but remember that it has a fat, chunky point that's hard to align with the ruler. The carbide is preferable for complicated layouts because it actually incises into the steel surface, and the intersection of two scribed lines can be felt by the sharp-pointed prick punch used to start a drill center. Not only felt, the trough formed will guide the punch point very accurately. The prick punch is very sharply pointed, and the center punch has a blunt, 45-degree angle point. Other than that, they are identical in appearance, so make sure you have a matching set, and use them in the correct sequence: prick first, center last.

A protective film is put on all shim stock to prevent corrosion, so to degrease the surface prior to spraying on layout dye, use lighter fluid, lacquer thinner, or naptha with a paper wipe. The layout dye dries almost instantly, especially if you put on a light coat, so don't overspray. As stated, the reason I recommend a spray layout dye — twenty or more pieces can be laid in order on a sheet of newspaper or on their respective paper sleeves and simultaneously marked. The dye keeps well and dries hard slowly, so extras may be stored for later processing. When I cut from different thicknesses of steel for experimental work, I remove each piece of steel from its skinny paper envelope, degrease it and place it back on top of the envelope so it masks the printed data. Then I spray the steel and when dry I resleeve it. At a glance, the dye marked envelope with pre-marked stock inside can be identified. If you are not storing them back in the envelope, wrap tissue around each one after drying. I will also mention that some people prefer to work with no layout dye at all. Instead they rely on the etched lines that the carbide scriber produces on the polished surface of the shim stock, remembering that a carbide point must be angled to align since it is so fat. The lines require correct lighting to see well, and I prefer instead layout dye, since a sharp-eyed operator can actually see a glimmering white line appear precisely at the point when the grinding wheel face begins to contact a scribed layout line on dye. With a second or two of grinding this white-appearing line disappears, which

signals that the layout line has been ground away. By watching for the white line, great initial accuracy and speed can be had. This is not as easy as it sounds, though, and a little practice will be in order.

For regular layout tasks you will need a depth gauge, a small machinist's rule, and an angle protractor. Clamp the steel blank into the vise edge-wise, and scribe the first line in Figure 9. Notice the inset. If the carbide point is held away from the ruler's edge, the line will be displaced from the real straightedge and inaccurate. If the ruler skids away from the surface being marked, the same thing will happen. To give the best accuracy, angle the scriber point into the ruler blade, and go so far as to clamp the ruler or protractor blade to the workpiece for critical layout jobs. The steel you are using is also very slippery to the scriber point, so be careful. A common machinist's trick for making two polished pieces of steel bind to each other is to insert some newspaper between them and tear or cut off the excess after clamping. The paper fibers are just abrasive enough to grip to the steel. To set the angle protractor for the correct depth easily, I've made a step gauge from some scrap ground flat stock. The tongue end of the ruler blade goes into the step and the baseplate of the protractor stays on the surface. This gauge can set the protractor to + or − .001 inches. Make sure all mating surfaces are flat and

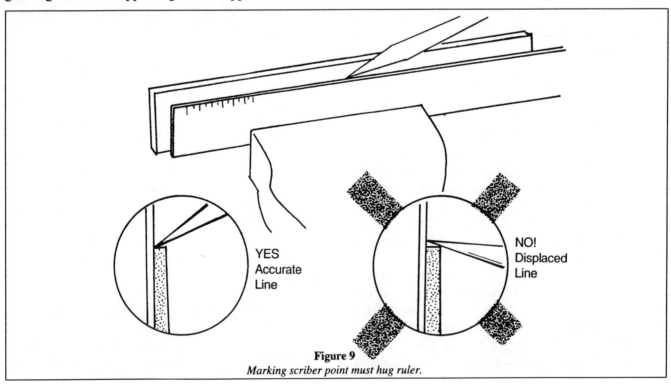

YES
Accurate
Line

NO!
Displaced
Line

Figure 9
Marking scriber point must hug ruler.

parallel when using this gauge to set the protractor, because even a slight tilt will seriously affect accuracy. Even though the operator can't grind to layout lines with the same accuracy the gauge can be set to, it's still good practice to layout as accurately as possible. The step gauge is labeled with the micrometer depth using a set of stamp letters and numbers and a hammer, or your carbide scriber. If other depths are needed, make a whole new gauge. For very small adjustments on these gauges that you will sneak up to one-thousandth at a time, use a mill file. If you become a convert to this system and agree that a gauge to set up every one of your pick-making operations is a good idea, pick up a couple of pounds of light aluminum in various flats and angles to make gauges with. It has excellent dimensional stability, and it is a snap to work with. Pick shank width is one such measurement it pays to set by gauge. If you have access to a drill press, a better jig can be made from a block of aluminum that is drilled and tapped for five or six holes. Each hole admits the narrow ruler tongue, and the slug threaded into the hole is a hex-head tap screw treated with Loctite to prevent creeping movement. The ruler can be set at different depths depending on where the screw is left in the hole. A slight change either way is easy to adjust. You might think the same jig executed in wood is as accurate, but it's not nearly as good. Only metal retains any sort of dimensional integrity. Wood is not an acceptable substitute, and although plastic is possible to work, I still prefer aluminum.

The flat ground style of tension wrench can be easily laid out on a piece of steel using the protractor-type depth gauge. This is also covered in the chapter on tension wrenches. The tongue is set to anywhere between 3 & 9 degrees, as per Figure 10 and the side of the gauge is aligned with the stock. Scribe one line, then slide the gauge down and scribe the next line. Now keep the setting and rotate the gauge 90 degrees so the end is aligned with the stock. Now the two wrench end lines can be scribed, making them match the side lines already done, and the width of wrench tip can be scribed last of all. Laying out the wrench in this fashion allows the maximum use of the stock, with minimum grinding time. In addition, the flat shank this configuration of wrench presents to the lock cylinder face permits it to be used on a lock that is set flush with its mounting surface. This is a good example of calculative layout since you don't know any of the dimensions exactly, you can only say that they are exactly 90 degrees in orientation. If you would like to calibrate the amount that you slide the protractor body over on the pick stock to scribe the second line that determines the width of the tension wrench body, set up as shown in Figure 11. The protractor body is slid over and butted up against the toolmaker's clamp, and then clamped in turn. Once the first line is scribed, loosen the clamp holding the protractor, and insert a gauge block between the protractor and the initial indexing clamp, then reclamp to scribe the second line.

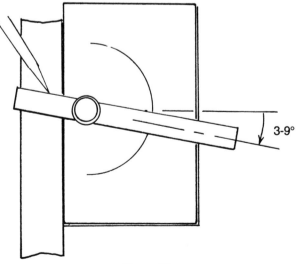

Figure 10
Using protractor gauge to scribe tension wrench cut lines to different angles.

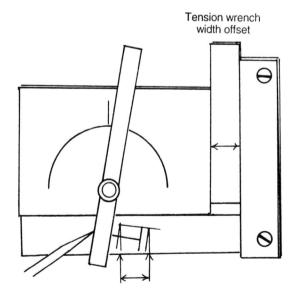

Figure 11
Layout of splayed-leg tension wrench using protractor and offset spacer.

What, you may ask, is a gauge block? Let's look at this valuable technique. Gauge blocks are pieces of metal that are very precisely finished in right angle, squareness and size. They are so perfect, in fact, that they can be made to cling together with almost molecular accuracy merely by hard pressure. This is called "wringing" a set of blocks together. This accuracy comes at a big price, so don't go out and get a set of gauge blocks, unless you buy a set of Chinese origin. You can use the next best thing, either a set of good quality shim feeler gauges, or a few odd sizes of ground flat stock. It is easy to see that a .010″ shim blade held next to a piece of flat ground stock that is .250″ will produce a gauge block offset of .260″. Various combinations of other pieces of metal will make up any size you desire, and with good repeatability. In the protractor set-off example at hand, a good initial try is for a .125″ dimension. There are formulas to tell you what that will translate out to in tension wrench shank width, but you get the idea. A known set-over produces layout lines that can be ground up to for a good approximation. Final finishing in conjunction with other measuring techniques will produce an accurate tool. Again, always try to work to greater precision than is required, if practical, since errors will inevitably affect the final tool.

I should mention that classical layout methods call for using dividers with needle sharp points that can be inserted into etched graduations on the 6″ rule. Once set they are used to scribe lines parallel to the long axis of the pick, one edge of the divider riding on the blank edge, the other divider leg doing the scribing. On slippery shim steel this is not at all easy to do accurately and requires a bit of practice, although it is very quick. The best approach is the use of gauge blocks acting on layout tools or against the working edges of the pick itself.

The term "working edge" also bears defining. On some classes of pick one edge is never touched, but is left smooth and straight as it comes from the factory. This is called the working edge and on our rake style lock pick tools it is usually the bottom.

For scribing angles, there is a tool produced from two pieces of shim stock. With a pop rivet or machine screw, secure the two pieces together by their drilled ends, and then slightly misalign the blades. The resulting angle can be measured if you wish, but all that is necessary to know is that an angle that produces the proper length of tension wrench and the proper width of shank is created. This angle can be preserved by clamping the set and then drilling another hole for another pop rivet. Both fasteners should obviously permit no movement in the two blades. If you have access to an acetylene torch the two pieces of steel can be brazed together permanently.

To use this jig, align the edge of the steel with one of the leg's edges, and scribe using the other leg as a straightedge. It will always be perfect from piece to piece. The small right-angled ends can be laid out almost by eye and checked with a small machinist's square as grinding progresses. In fact, in Figure 12, a design for a splayed-leg tension wrench shows that a right angle is not always a good design for a multi-end tool. This design allows the necessary clearance between tension wrench shank and lock cylinder/door face, yet it uses the steel to good economy.

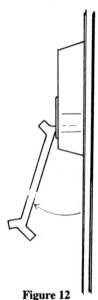

Figure 12
Note splayed-leg puts working end of wrench away from lock mount surface.

Let me go on record as saying that I cannot stand those double-ended picks personally. The typical tool has a lifter on one end and a diamond on the other end. It makes the shank much smaller and is difficult to shift end-for-end while holding the tension wrench on. Furthermore, it usually spells trouble big time when you have to shift from raking to lifting and back again a couple of times. My instructions to apprentices are to start over again if one stint of raking during a lifting attack won't turn the trick. The double-ended lock pick is an example in frustration but they look real "CIA" so they crop up a lot. They are undeniably cool, if impractical, tools.

On the other side of the coin I am strongly in favor of double-, triple-, quadruple-ended tension wrenches. Consider this. Make a wrench that has four identical ends with varying widths. Start with the narrowest and go to the next up and so on until one wedges tightly. This is very easy with a multiple-ended tool. One grab will get you four tools, and it also saves a lot of bulk. It's harder to juggle four separate tools in and out of your case.

Eddie will now set the wayback machine and talk about his early exploits making lock picks. The first lock pick book I got had a few fuzzy pictures of several lock picks with various ends. Here was knowledge and power waiting within my grasp if only I could duplicate those angles and shapes. After going nowhere with the magnifying glass I finally drew lots of complicated lines and stuff right on the book in an attempt to duplicate the pick tips on actual steel. All that got me was a bunch of numbers I was not tooled up to use then. I was disturbed to find out that water will quickly trash a paper pattern glued to a lock pick being ground and quenched repeatedly.

As eddie's technique matured lock pick pictures in books became unimportant. In the end eddie started to decide how the pick should be shaped. Let me ask you some questions: who decides exactly how a lock pick will be laid out? Who says how much of a curve it will have at the end (if a lifter) and how high the diamond will be? The answer is the lock, if you can learn how to make it talk to you. You can, by actually measuring and figuring, design which will be the most perfect shape for opening a given lock. Eddie will teach you how to do the two types, lifter and diamond.

The classical diamond pick shape is meant to be used to rake the lock. It relies on its ability to "billiard ball" the tumblers. To make a diamond ideal for a given lock, you need only measure a key that fits a lock of that type. If you don't have a key or lock of that type, other approaches will be discussed later, but now back to the key.

You will need a measuring tool; ideally the dial calipers, or at least an engraved ruler. First examine the key to locate the shoulder. Every key has a right angle shoulder that hits part of the lock keyway and regulates precisely how far the key can be inserted, so that the key bitting lines up exactly with the tumblers. Locate any such discernible shoulder or key to the

lock stop located at the bow end of the key. Measure from there to the exact middle of the bottom of the furthest key bitting cut. This measurement is the working length the pick shank and tip needs to be to penetrate far enough into the lock keyway to reach all the tumblers. Next measure the distance between any two consecutive key bitting cuts. This will be the pin-to-pin spacing. The distance two pins are apart is very important since it indicates the point at which the pick shank can safely rise to become the pick nose or tip. If the shank raises too soon it will also act on the adjacent pin, which is very bad if you don't want to move two pins at the same time. Finally, grab that pencil you used to write down this lock's vital statistics. While holding it normally, measure how much of the pencil is in the hand. This will be a guide for how much pick handle you will be comfortable with initially. You may modify this number up or down as your technique progresses. Your measurements are: a) length in lock pick; b) pin spacing; c) length of handle. You can make an extreme fuss over measuring the angle of the key bitting cuts. The official number is 50 degrees, but eddie uses 45 degrees and it works just fine. It also means that any diamond you cut has equal force on it in and out. From these measurements it is easy to lay out your first actual pick. Use a foot long piece of ½″ wide .031″ shim stock covered in layout blue. Scribe a line using a square at the approximate center of the steel. This is the lock face parting line. Set your dividers to the "a" figure plus an $^1/_8$″ (for fudging). Use the dividers to scribe a line as in Figure 13, and scribe a line 45 degrees away facing out from that point. Now at this point normally you would flip the protractor and scribe one more 45 degree line facing in, to complete the diamond shape. The problem is, how high to make the diamond? How far away does the second 45 degree line go? To answer that question we must go back to the lock again.

At this point examine the key from your sample lock. It may have cuts that are the same height as the next or adjacent cut. It may have some slightly lower or higher than the adjacent cut. What you are looking for is the biggest difference in height between adjacent bitting cuts. There is a maximum allowable height variation between two adjacent cuts. This restriction is necessary to maintain the bottoms or "vees" of the cuts in line with the tumblers. An excessively deep or high cut would intrude into the space reserved for the adjacent cut, and leave the

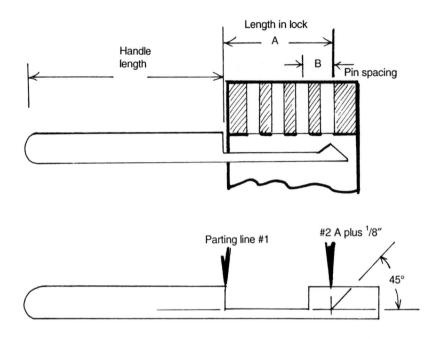

Figure 13
Initial layout for diamond pick.

adjacent tumbler end riding on the too deep/high cut's slope. See Figure 14. This maximum allowable cut height is also the most that your diamond height should be. It may of course be a lot less, but the higher the diamond the more energy imparted to the pins during a rake opening. The same principle applies to the classical lifter layout. If you want to avoid measuring the maximum allowed cut, just find it (if it exists on the key) and trace it directly into the layout dye on the pick blank. Orient the key shank parallel to the pick axis when doing this. The same "trace directly from key technique" works for quick and dirty snake or profile pick layout creation, since the heights and spacing are already cut machine correct. Finally, remember we said the maximum allowable. If you want your diamonds cut down in height, merely continue to grind PAST the layout point to adjust diamond height. This can be done any time after the pick is in use as well. The only rule is to keep the angle the same. Within about 2-3 degrees is close enough. Having discussed the diamond, eddie will now move on to the lifter. Here is where your tool really begins to differ from the commercial jobs. I have no idea who initially designed that clunky lifter profile, but like the boss told the strip-bar applicant, "Way too fat for pro work."

The classical lifter pick layout ideally has two curves in it, the end of the lifter and the shank. The curve is a quarter or less part of a circle, and the diameter of the circle is such that the point of the tumbler adjacent to the tumbler being manipulated will rest on the exact spot on the pick shank where the curve begins to sweep up from the width of the pick shank. This will ensure that the adjacent picked tumblers will not be affected or overlifted by the tool's working tip as it moves around in the lock. In theory, the maximum height difference allowed between two drivers should also enter into the calculation, but it is always less important than the previous dimension. To calculate the diameter of the pick tip upsweep radius, measure the outside of two adjacent pin wells as in Figure 15. From this dimension subtract one pin tumbler diameter (usually .115" or .120") and the result will be the center-to-center distance between adjacent drivers. That figure is also the diameter of hole that you want to layout on the pick stock. My data tallies have over twenty different makes of lock to distill, and the average seems to be .160" which is very close to $^5/_{32}$" drill size, or can be bracketed by a drill size #20 or #21.

There are radius gauges available in different sizes that can be used to trace with, but there is a more precise method. Once the number is calculated, select whatever number drill comes closest to the micrometer number, and, using this drill, shoot a hole into a piece of .015" brass stock. This negative hole created from a positive drill rod now becomes the tracing template to use for the radius. Clamp this template down, and insert the tip of your carbide scriber into the hole, pushing it outward till it contacts the edge of the circle. The selection of very thin sheet brass for the template makes holding an accurate scribing angle much easier. Place a straightedge alongside the hole and nudge it inward until it contacts the scriber point. The straightedge will then be perfectly tangential to the hole. Scribe a layout line as shown in Figure 16 and grind along this to cut out the template required. This template may then be aligned either to another layout line on the blank or physically aligned with a semi-finished pick. Scribe the remaining layout lines and grind as close to them as possible. If you are seduced by all those double-half and full-ball and diamond shape picks used for raking a lock open, this same layout method will make their templates also, and with great accuracy. The procedure is to scribe a line on the aluminum stock, and, using a center punch and hammer, make a center prick mark exactly on it. From this center (not *in* the center of the stock at all) prick draw a circle with dividers set to the pin well center-to-center distance. Do another center prick where the circle crosses the line. Two holes will be drilled in these centers; the diameter of the hole is up to you.

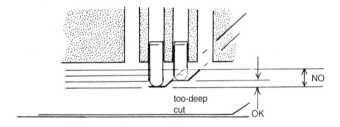

Figure 14
Notice that key cuts that are so deep they remove material from adjacent pin key areas are forbidden!

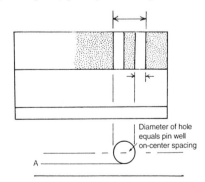

Figure 15
Shows line "A" scribed tangential to hole to form lifter hook profile.

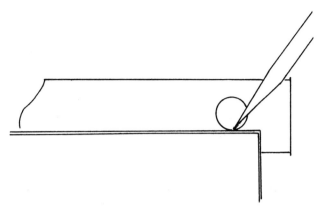

Figure 16
Method of scribing line tangentially to drilled hole.

The largest diameter is of course the maximum difference in height between two adjacent drivers. Usually this figure is .030″, but it may be looked up in a code book or measured and calculated from the right key bitting combination. One very common practice is to make the first ball (which will be cut from lines traced from the hole drilled) the maximum height difference, and the second ball the minimum step. The position of the balls (holes) may be switched, and even three, four, or five holes can be drilled. By the way, this layout method is also the easiest way by far to generate the complex wiggly pick outlines some pick artists still swear by. Once the wiggly outline has been generated, it may be further modified before the actual cutting commences. To return to the ball pick, after the holes are drilled, the template is finished by grinding away half the template to the initial line. The template may then be lined up flush with either an existing layout line or another semi-finished pick shank. It is crucial to remember that to produce a double-balled pick the grind must be modified to put the shank UP from the usual base of the tool. If this is not done, there will be no steel to make the lower set of half balls from, yes? With multiple sets of ball templates, one can be used for upper and one for lower tracing. The template can be flipped to exchange the order of the balls on the shank. A diamond on the bottom, a ball on top; the combinations involved are many. Let me also go on record here as saying that I have a low opinion of the wiggly pick, the vaunted "king and queen" pick, and the rake pick with tip modified from a diamond shape. The theory of raking is, of course, to impart the billiard ball transfer of shock from the lower pin to the upper pin, but rounding the point of the diamond will also reduce the reverse shock and/or acceleration of the driver to less than that maximum. It may be great fun to have all those geometric shapes, but it won't open locks any faster or better than raking skill with a single diamond. The wiggly or multiple profile pick has a different principle of operation. It is intended to align multiple drivers simultaneously, which is supposedly useful if tolerances are very tight and picking is especially difficult. The wiggly pick pretends to be the right key in essence. The real problem is that the higher tolerance the lock, the larger the number of possible combinations of key that will NOT fit.

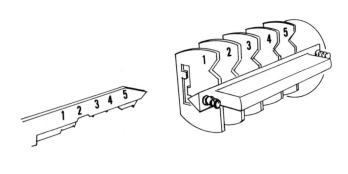

Figure 17
Automotive disc lock showing sidebar system.

Let me explain this in detail. You can figure out how many steps in the key system, how many drivers or tumblers, and use that data to computer generate a list of all possible combinations like 1111, 1112, 1113, 1121, 1131, and so forth. Then, like trying to "box" THE LOTTERY NUMBER, you can attempt to come up with several pick combinations or profiles that match probable ones on your listing. The commercially available models claim to have done just that. Just consider the tolerance of the lock. If the steps/increments of key bitting are .007″, but the driver will catch if the key is .003″ off either high or low, then there is in effect a set of "half" numbers or combinations that if picked to, will do absolutely nothing. This is why I say the number of WRONG

combinations is a lot larger than just the code possibilities.

The wiggly pick got its start from the automotive lock industry. An automotive lock with a sidebar set into the plug and shell will prevent applying pressure on the wafers, or discs of the lock until ALL of them are almost in line. The wiggly pick was supposed to act like a surrogate key and ALMOST line up all the wafers simultaneously because of sloppy tolerances, and the sidebar would begin to snap in. Even better (or worse depending on your viewpoint), the sidebar has to be spring loaded to snap IN to the shell, and it actually helps line up tumblers that are almost in position. See the accompanying Figure 17.

Sets of automotive try-out keys that were available in the 1950-1963 period relied on this same fact. The difference there was that the tolerance of the locks then being produced closely approached the bitting depths, and keys cut to a half depth could thereby bridge the gap and work two combinations simultaneously. The number of combinations went down so dramatically that by using 50 keys and wiggling each one around, one would effect an opening. The wiggly or wiggly pick comes from that same period in locksmithing history. The wiggly pick still is valuable for automotive locksmithing today, but I believe that any opening on a pin tumbler residential lockset effected with such a tool could have been just as easily done with a single lifter pick. Remember that the single lifter perfectly duplicates the action of the key, as far as each single dumb driver knows, so the lifter comes closest to masquerading as the actual key.

The layout procedures eddie teaches here may seem to be way too fussy for you, but consider two points. First, each layout only needs to be done well once, because second generation picks may be directly traced from the first tool onto a new blank. Secondly, the time will come when you'll need to make a pick that is EXACTLY such-and-such high with so-and-so clearance, and when that day comes, having secure layout and measuring technique under your fingertips will save the day.

For other comments on rough layout technique, also see the chapter on rough grinding, and the chapter on tension wrenches.

Chapter Five
Initial Layout

This chapter deals with the first steps of whittling away metal to get to a finished pick. Your completed rough-ground pick should look like Figure 18. Notice that the working length of the shank will remain nearly the same after finish grinding, while the height and contours of the working tip will be much altered after finishing. To lay out the cutting guide lines for this first step use a surface gauge, or a preset scribing gauge to produce the parallel lines. A surface gauge is a block of metal with a lapped flat bottom and sides, and a double-jointed arm that terminates with a pointed scriber. Most surface gauges have a set screw for fine adjustment as well. To set it initially put an engraved 6″ ruler end-up on a sheet of glass, and set the pointer so it precisely "clicks" into whatever engraved mark you are using for approximate pick shank width.

Figure 18
All-purpose pick blank.

When selecting a 6″ ruler make sure the graduations are engraved (cut by machine into the steel) and not just printed or etched on. For precise setting of small pick widths, the ruler is available in graduations of 100 per inch. This is called a 16R scale in the trade. Once the height gauge is accurately

set, place it and the pick stock on edge upon a piece of glass and move the tip of the scriber along the pick at an angle. It will describe a perfectly parallel line on the layout dye sprayed on the pick stock. To keep the pick stock at 90 degrees you can back it up with a small machinist's square or anything reasonably cube-like. The same square will produce the right angle layout lines (end lines) also needed on the pick blank.

If you don't feel the need to get this accurate, the pick stock or blank covered with layout dye can be dropped in the slot you cut into your bench pin, and the line scribed along the surface of the pin. Not as good, but serviceable. It will just require a little more care in rough grinding, since you shouldn't go right up to the line.

As I said, a square or surface gauge will produce the end line, or you can make a one-step tracing jig as outlined below. Be sure to scribe a set of arrowheads whose points stop or cross on the length line once you put cut lines in. These arrows are scribed in the area of the pick that will be ground away. This prevents cutting the opposite side by mistake, and allows the eye to pick up the length line easier, since it will not show up well in light angled to show up the width line instead.

For one-step scribing of rough layout lines, I will show you the aluminum jig used for years at my shop. To make this jig, procure a piece of aluminum angle 1″ x 1″ x $^1/_8$″ and 6″ long. Aluminum is very easy to work and therefore ideal for jigs that only involve tracing or marking. Hold a finished rough-ground pick into the bottom of this angle as in Figure 19 and secure it with a couple of machinist's clamps. Now scribe the outline of the ground steel pick onto the aluminum inner face of the angle. Remove the pick and take the aluminum to the bandsaw/bench wheel and cut or grind out the profile you traced, paying strict attention to accuracy. Saw a little short of the line and finish up by filing or belt grinding. Filing will be very slow and tedious since the file will have to be cleaned of the numerous aluminum chips frequently. That's why the jig should be band-sawn. A belt grinder will be a lot faster than filing for the final working.

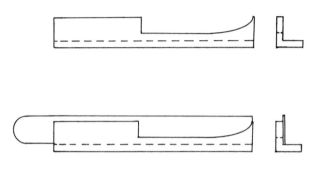

Figure 19
*Blank pick inserted in marking jig
to scribe final cut lines.*

Once this master tracing jig is made, any number of chisel-cut half, third, or coil blanks can be quickly scribed with the profile required and then taken to the grinding wheel immediately. I omit the use of layout dye if the tracing procedure is followed, since with a carbide-tipped tool, the lines can be scribed deep enough to discern under the light easily. One pass is deep enough, even with a light touch. When marking with this method beginners have a tendency to re-scribe over the same line to make a deeper impression, but any repeat scribing rarely follows the exact same path each time, and only makes the layout line fatter. A really fat layout line seriously decreases accuracy of the grind since it increases the "correct" or "safe" area the grinder is trying to grind to. A heavy touch may cause the scriber to skip or slip away out of control, so go lightly. As an exercise see how light a line you can scribe, and then grind to it.

This aluminum jig may also be later modified incrementally by filing or belt grinding if it is decided that more material should be customarily removed during the rough grinding. When removing more metal from this marking jig, take care that it will still always produce a rough pick that is truly universal in that its contours can be made into any type of pick

without being "short" some steel. If you remove too much material the jig will always mark "short" and must then be replaced or make-do modified to something else like a final profile marking jig. If in doubt, before you start any cutting on the original, use a rough blank made from the starting master jig to make a second generation jig and use it for experiment.

Once the blank is lined you go right to the wheel, check it for cracks or flaws, turn on the mist, dress the wheel, and go. The speed of the grind is of some importance here. By speed, I don't mean the wheel's rpm's but rather the rate at which the steel is fed into the wheel. Since it is technically a roughing-in operation you should go as fast as possible, but it is possible to feed so fast that even the mist coolant bath will not stay ahead of the heat generated. By close observation of the pattern of coolant flow on the face of the steel you can detect any areas of steel that become heated enough to vaporize the coolant. These hot spots will be potential danger areas if grinding speed and temp increase any further. For your first few tries start out slowly, then gradually increase the feed speed. The coolant will start to avoid areas of the pick in contact with the wheel, but this is still okay. At some faster feed point you may notice the sudden "blooming" of the tell-tale blue oxidation color. It will be seen to bleed away from the grind line into the main steel body. When this occurs, immediately lower pressure on the wheel and the temperature will cool below the danger point. Now, by slow and careful grinding, that small bloom of untempered steel can be removed and grinding then resumed at a new rate reasonably below danger levels. Remember to adjust the coolant spray direction so it will be exactly on the region where steel meets wheel, not on the wheel itself. A little experience will let you know how fast to rough-grind a piece. The real quick guy can push a line of blue discoloration almost all the way to the scribed line, and then back off the feed speed at just the proper moment and end up with a perfectly good expanse of steel. The even faster guy knows that the steel that will be ground off later in final profiling can also be left burnt and it won't matter. I prefer to leave no such blue in the rough grind, because in very small picks there seems to be a subtle alteration of the steel chemistry in the zone surrounding the tell-tale blue discoloration. I grind a little slower and have better results. The difference in pushing the line and staying conservative is negligible in most cases anyway, especially if the wheel is frequently dressed so it runs cooler.

Notice that when you grind off those little tabs of steel before going to the next cut, they heat up much quicker? That is because of their small mass. The rule is the smaller the piece, the slower it should be ground, even with that nifty mist coolant set-up!

As a rule of thumb, a ¾″ full cut in .028-.035″ shim stock to a depth of ¼″ should take no more than 45 seconds with no overheating. If you find that you are taking a lot longer than this, even as much as six minutes, something is very wrong and you should check on a couple of factors. Make sure the coolant spray pattern is centered on the steel, not the face of the grinding wheel. Check that the amount of coolant being sprayed is adequate and that the atomization is complete. If you are uncertain about either of these, try both to increase the air pressure and open the flow needle valve more. Since coolant is cheap, use as much as you want!

The most common factor to look for in excessive heat buildup is a glazed surface on the grinding wheel face. In nine times out of ten the wheel needs to be dressed. Between a dressed and a glazed wheel we are talking 45 seconds versus 3 minutes, and mucho added heat. The more glaze, the more heat and the less cut. Glazing will happen to you as you use the wheel normally. The glaze is composed of worn stone and particles of stones and steel, and even binder from the wheel. A telltale sign of this glaze is the volume of sparks given off during the grinding, and the amount of heat transferred through into the handle of the lock pick. If the amount of sparks is very low and the handle heat is very high, then the wheel surface is badly glazed and should be redressed immediately. Another indicator of a glazed wheel is an untrue or wavy grind. A further good indicator of glaze is a darker line on the wheel that produces a persistent "hot spot" on the pick steel. If in doubt, always try redressing the wheel since this will frequently work wonders!

It is smart practice to monitor constantly the speed of rough grinding and redress when any falloff in performance is detected. Without a fresh wheel surface, the coolant set-up is really inadequate to the potential heat buildup. Redressing the wheel takes only ten seconds or so, and is never the wrong thing to do. Wheels should be treated as a perishable item.

One or at most two wheel face width bites will get you over to the relief line. Once it is reached,

reverse the pick end-for-end (if you are working on the left–hand wheel as I customarily do) and angle the pick 45 degrees to do the relief cut. Cut in until the radius of the wheel edge just matches the bottom of the straight cut, and then stop. Have a thick rag or wooden dowel handy to wipe off the splinters. Large amounts of free steel splinters await you on the down side (now the top side) of the pick. The ones still attached can be ground off with a very light touch as in Figure 20 as long as you don't dig into polished areas. They can also be filed off later, if you are timid about using the wheel. I myself strike off the bulk of these splinters with the wooden stick I use to feed and control the pick steel. I will explain about the stick.

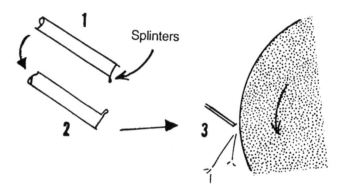

Figure 20
*Lightly cutting off surplus splinters
left from rough grinding.*

Some extra aid in holding is really essential for anyone who plans to grind more than just one or two tools. It may not seem like too much trouble to hold the steel in your bare hands, but the many slivers and burrs created by the grinding process and left on the tool will eventually leave your hands with dozens of small cuts. Those freshly created wire edges are very sharp and will cut deeply if impelled by a slip at the wheel. Some form of holding is also safe practice in avoiding "kickbacks" and plain accidents of all types. The grinding coolant mist will also make your hold very slippery, and long exposure to coolant is hard on the hands.

The best type of protection is a piece of wood dowel that you hold in your left hand and which the lefthand edge of the tool digs into. This is more secure for holding than it sounds, and this is the method I habitually use for hand grinding to perimeter lines. The right hand holds the bare steel, and the left holds the short length of dowel angling up into the corner of the tool from below. The dowel has a hole ¼″ diameter drilled an inch deep into its end to hold and trap the pick tip. This wood dowel both damps vibrations, holds, and also pushes the tool into the wheel. It works especially well for me since I always grind with the tool handle at the left and the working tip at the right, with the lefthand wheel set up for grinding.

That's all there is to the roughing out. If you are trying to put blanks ahead and will store them for several days or longer, either drop them into a light oil bath to prevent rust, or heat them well and then apply a little WD-40 or Starrett M-1 spray, again for rust. The mist coolant must be neutralized since it is mostly water.

Chapter Six
Grinding at The Wheel

Grinding is the easiest technique available to work thin pieces of hardened lock pick steel as is, meaning without annealing or softening. If you grind right to the layout line, the wheel leaves a surface finish that will require only a little file work for completion. If any attempt was made to cut shim stock using a saw, for example, the cut would be very tedious due to the hardness of the metal, with frequent breakage of the blade as well. By comparison, grinding takes but a few minutes.

It will help you to explore briefly the cutting action of a grinding wheel. The wheel is composed mostly of abrasive minerals. The grain size and hardness are matched to the material the wheel is designed to cut. The abrasive grains are formed into a hard wheel by mixing them with substances that solidify under very high heat. The wheel is actually baked in a kiln.

The abrasive grains in the wheel are not round in shape, they are really square-, diamond-, or otherwise angularly shaped. As a result of the natural crystal-like shape, each grain has a sharp cutting edge. Taken together, these millions of tiny cutting edges are able to bite into whatever is being ground, even the hardest high-carbon steel. As their edges cut or chisel the metal away, they also blunt and fracture, eventually flaking away from the binder. A grinding wheel will therefore groove and use itself up as it is worked. It must be frequently re-formed or dressed to produce a straight cut again. The dressing process also removes leftover pieces of whatever material is being ground, and blunts packed-in grains. A wheel clogged with this junk cuts poorly and also heats up rapidly from the excessive friction generated. The term for this clogging is a "glazed" wheel.

Dressing restores the surface by removing the glaze and also retruing the surface to flat. Two main types of dressing tools are a toothed star wheel, which is mounted in a special holder, and an industrial diamond pointing tool. The diamond is intended for precision applications, and is valuable only for precise profiling of a wheel, like a precise radius on the corner for lifters. The more common tool is the star wheel. This has a pack of five or six wheels with multiple points of hardened steel. These star points can break off grains without being excessively ground down while doing so. The stars avoid wear because they wheel around rapidly, and because solid discs in the wheel pack prevent the dresser from digging in too deeply.

Dressing a wheel with a star is classified as a hazardous operation, requiring precautions. Always read and follow the grinding wheel manufacturer's instructions relating to wheel dressing. Wear eye protection at all times. The dressing star MUST be firmly seated on the grinding wheel's rest. If the rest is missing, do not attempt to dress the wheel, as dangerous kickback will result. Kickback may result in serious personal injury or even death. This is because dressing may cause a wheel to fracture. A fractured wheel turning at high speeds will literally explode, so work safely. You ain't NEVER been stoned like that!

To dress a wheel, apply the star pack very lightly against the stone at the point you normally grind, until the wheel face is true again. It will chatter and buzz as it whirls, and give off the occasional spark, and this is all normal. Some grains, grit and dust will be whirled off, and this is normal also.

Some minor profiling can also be done with a star by rounding a corner of the wheel to match the radius needed for a tool like the lifter pick. Eventually the teeth of the star will disappear and can be replaced. When you replace the star wheel pack, remember that one side of the nut assembly holding the steel axle pin in the cast holder is a lefthand thread.

Safety in using and mounting grinding wheels is nothing to laugh at. Getting brained with a small brick traveling at motor-driven velocity is one of the more serious-type accidents. There are some rules to follow:

1. If the motor shaft and the wheel hole don't match, make sure to use an approved arbor or bushing. Some wheels come with a variety of these included.

2. To prevent over-tightening and stressing the wheel, make and use a pair of cardboard washers between both sides of the wheel and the steel holding washers, as in Figure 21.

3. When starting a new wheel, plug the grinder in from a remote location and let the new wheel run unattended for an entire 15 minute espresso (eddie don't do coffee) break. Any hidden flaws will show up by then, and a wheel that may put on a deadly missile show will do so for an empty house.

4. After running a new wheel for 1 to 5 minutes, dismount it from the grinder and suspend it by a string through the hole. A very light tap on the wheel with a screwdriver handle may indicate if any hidden flaws and cracks exist. A good wheel usually gives a high-pitched sound and a bad wheel sounds dull or dead. This test should be applied at periodic intervals to monitor the health of the wheel. If in doubt about a particular wheel, discard it. They are not expensive compared to teeth.

5. Always follow the manufacturer's recommendations for care, mounting, nut tightening, and use of any specific abrasive wheel.

What kind of wheel to use? Avoid the dime-store shaft-mounted stones. Buy only a wheel that has a hole for arbor mounting. As you may know, the industrial supply houses carry specialty wheels for exotic steels or other materials, but frequently they require a large arbor and/or large machine to run. The standard bench grinder arbor shaft size is $^1/_2''$ or $^5/_8''$.

If you can get a soft stone that will mount on your bench grinder assembly, that is good. The softer stone will wear a lot faster because the abrasive grains are flaking away rapidly. This has the effect of making the grind go a lot quicker and a little cooler as well. Nothing happens for nothing however, but the trade-off in the wearing and more frequent redressing and wheel replacement is well worth it.

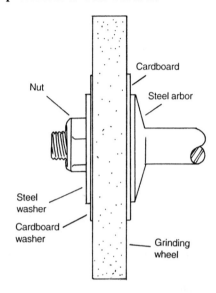

Figure 21
Recommended grinding wheel mounting using cardboard washers.

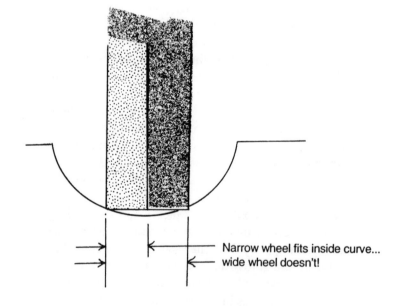

Figure 22
To grind inside curves, thinner width is better.

The much-quoted rule is hard wheels for soft materials and soft wheels for hard materials. The common aluminum oxide wheel is fine for your pick tool grinding. The larger the face width, the fewer grinding passes will have to be done while roughing out a tool, so try for a ¾" width. With a very long arbor, multiple wheels can be side-to-side mounted for even greater face width, if the wheel manufacturer expressly states this can be done. For grinding the insides of curves, the smaller the width the better. Look at Figure 22 for an example of this curve-fitting rule. If you mount any wheel or combination of wheel surfaces wider than ¾", you should add a second coolant nozzle to cover the extra width. Not only will more wheel in contact with the steel produce much more heat, but the spray pattern will be insufficient to cover all areas of the pick. Most spray coolant units have a two-nozzle system available for a few dollars more than a single unit. Truth is, a ¾" wheel will handle most pick grind jobs.

The important aspect of the cooling mist is not only that water is applied to the steel, but also that the mist is constantly replacing the heated water with cooler water, and at a faster rate than even a stream of water could do. While we look at spray patterns, a little experimentation while seated at the wheel will show you that a pattern directed too much at the wheel surface and not more directly at the steel will cause large quantities of the coolant to be hurled into the air at a right angle to the wheel. This deluge of mist will soon wet down the guy doing the grinding. Aiming a little more directly at the steel will reduce this mist thrown off to almost zero. Once the proper position is found, mark it for future reference. This will also help you to keep the stock in the spray pattern. Stock that is held too close or far from the spray pattern will overheat and burn, so monitor this closely.

Do not grind in the same room where you do any bench and assembly work, because the grains given off will lodge in any greased working surface on a lock and cause excessive accuracy-destroying wear! If you must, put a tarp over the bench and lay down some wet newspaper on the floor to catch the abrasive dust/mist. Don't slip or trip on the wet newspaper and fall against the grinder. I wear sneakers while grinding.

Once the layout lines have been completed, grinding may begin according to your set sequence. The first roughing cut should be even with the end of the tool, and should be carried down almost to the layout lines that delineate the height of the tip. By

contrast, if you decided to make the first cut where the handle begins, the heat built up by the grinding would have two places to go, to the handle and to the tip. Now, heat flowing into the handle is good for a cool grind, because the handle has lots of mass and surface area and therefore can absorb a lot of heat before it will begin to lose temper. In practice I have never seen a handle untemper. The problems would begin to start when the first roughing grind had been completed. The extremely small cross-section of the tool shank would prevent any more heat from rapidly flowing into the handle, and on the next cut practically all the heat would concentrate in the tip area, where the mass is less than the handle, and would only get much lesser as the grind progresses. The result is more heat build-up. That is why the desired approach is a grind progressing from the extreme tip back to the handle, allowing more heat to escape through fewer "bottlenecks."

We were doing a grind at the tip straight down to the layout lines. Once this first cut is completed you can jump over one wheel width and start over. Notice that at some point the grinding wheel will have metal on both sides bumping or striking against the sides of the wheel. It is crucial to realize the potential for disaster here. If the wheel catches its side against the tool and draws the tool down, the cut's width clearance will narrow until the opposite side of the wheel will catch also and wedge or tighten! Once that happens the wheel will whip the tool from your grasp, and turn it into a sharp-edged missile. To prevent this it is tempting to push the steel against the *side* of the wheel and grind some additional clearance, but avoid this. The side of the wheel is like a block wall. Straight up and down the wall is very strong in compression, but side to side it's very weak in tension. Grinding wheels can shear and break if repeatedly stressed on the sides. Instead of this, just shift the cut when the amount of cut penetration amounts to over $^1/_{16}$". Go to the next cut position, cut $^1/_{16}$" deep, then shift back for another bite. It's maybe slower going but it is much safer. It is advisable to leave a tiny tab between these cuts which will help "center" the cut and prevent the steel walking over sideways and making an angle cut. The small tab can be quickly ground off before the next cut sequence. Also try to avoid a "knocking" cut that just catches the corner of the wheel and walks down it. The sharp edge of the wheel is excellent for this because it breaks down so rapidly. The problem is that a that a severely rounded edge has to be dressed true again by losing a lot of good face that is relatively untouched, so use the full cutting face of the wheel evenly and it will last longer. The only advantage of a severely rounded wheel edge is that the catching effect is reduced a little, but don't count on this.

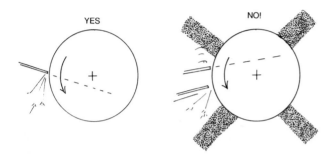

Figure 23
*The work piece should always point
below the center of the wheel.*

The "whipping" or catching effect that a wheel has on a tight plunge roughing cut will also occur in a pushing out direction if the steel is held at an UP angle to the face of the grinding wheel as in Figure 23. There should always be a greater than 90-degree angle between the face of the wheel leaving the cut steel, and the width of the steel shim, and a less than 90-degree angle between the surface of the wheel approaching the cut area, and the width of the steel shim. As the steel approaches the wheel it can become caught, and will whip away at great speed and inertia. The force comes from the motor itself and its torque. Study Figure 23 carefully so you understand which is the right way and which is the wrong way!

Remember to mount and break in your grinding wheels according to manufacturer's recommendations, plan your cut sequences carefully to avoid dangerous heat build-up, and observe safe cutting angles when holding or setting up work to be ground.

Chapter Seven
Grinding Coolant Methods

In this chapter eddie discourses on mist coolant, an idea which will save you tens of hours by producing cooler, faster pick grinding. The professional lock pick builder will never be able to experiment with new designs if each new pick takes an hour to rough out. Eddie does it in six minutes with mist or drip coolants.

Tell the truth now, how many picks can you cut on the wheel in an hour without burning one or two? Grinding a pick to its perimeter shape requires the removing of very little actual metal, only about twenty percent or so of the total tool blank. The catch is in the tempered hardness of the metal. Don't get me wrong, because this hardness, created by carefully controlled heat-treating, creates a tool that is quite resistant to bending in very small cross-sections. The more bend resistance there is, the smaller the tool can be while still remaining capable of transferring enough necessary pressure from the tool user's hand to the lock tumblers. I will take all the toughness I can get and be happy for it, but it does mean that grinding this same metal produces friction, and friction makes heat.

So much heat is produced by the process of the grind that it can travel along the metal and untemper or anneal the pick you are trying to work on. It will anneal faster than the grind can proceed. That's sure not good, because the pick cannot be easily restored to its former precision degree of temper. Only a whole benchload of heat-treat equipment and the know-how to use them can bring the temper back with precision. It also takes time to re-temper, and may alter the chemical alloy makeup.

The practical way is to avoid annealing the pick in the first place, and you will do this by preventing that excess heat from building up enough in temperature to ruin your pick.

The quick and easy way is to just dip the steel into a can full of water very frequently. This is so common a method that many pedestal grinders are provided with a plastic or cast metal cup to hold water at the grinder. Since this method means lots of trips between the grinder wheel and the water tub, it pays to position the tub no further than 6″ from the wheel, preferably below the wheel. A wide-mouthed shallow tub will help too, since both the hand holding the pick and the pick itself are allowed quick in and out access. The initial rough cuts will be full wheel-face ones, and will generate the most amount of heat. Since they must chew up the most steel real estate, they will take a lot of time too. For this first step then, a rhythm of grind, dip, swirl-in-the-water, and back-to-the-wheel helps to speed the process. A favorite eddie trick is to find a good R & B radio station and nail a tune that matches your work pace. Get a copy of that tune. The more time spent on the wheel and the less in the air or the water, the quicker you get done, so get a system.

For just a few tools a water tub will work fine, but a practicing lock pick artist will design over five tools a week initially, and at three to five variations of each pick this adds up to a lot of drudgery at the wheel. The heat build up from grinding is so very rapid, in relation to the mass of steel available to absorb that heat, that most of the time spent standing at the grinding wheel will be taken up in removing, cooling, and carefully re-dressing the steel to the grinding wheel. The ultimate easy answer is coolant grinding. Don't take my word for it, just try making one pick using the water pot and you will wind up thinking there has to be an easier way. There is and the old-time peddler has already done it.

Adding a simple coolant system to the lowly tabletop grinding wheel setup is really quite easy. In times gone by that streetcart knife sharpener used an empty tomato can of water with a hole punched in the bottom for a steady drip-drip-drip. The can was hung over the large foot driven grinding wheel so that it deposited water right where the blade was applied to the wheel. The water also lubricated and carried away particles of steel that would have clogged the grinding stone's pores. The old tin can dodge still works today. A couple of holes nail–punched at the top rim will hold a wire loop. The wire loop is hung on a hanger wire (the good stiff kind, not today's cheap variety) for easy removal. The can's drip hole is sized according to your needs. The can is dip-filled from a large basin placed nearby the workbench. The free length of wire trailing from the loop in one side can be inserted down in the water and through the drip hole. It's still attached so it won't fall through. This wire can be bent so that it's positioned just above where the drip should go, and it will lead the water down with precision.

For a lot of water, one of those institutional size cans can easily be adapted to your bench grinder. Haul one out of the trash during the next restaurant call you make, and have it washed. You will also need a two-foot length of ¼″ outside diameter copper tubing, and some plumbing solder and flux. Back at the shop, drill a ¼″ hole in the side of the can about one-half inch above the bottom. Insert one end of the copper tubing into the middle of the can and put this assembly on a fire brick or fireproof surface on your bench. Apply flux and then solder. Check for leaks at the solder joint after a little cooling. This can filled with water is HEAVY so it must be placed on a shelf or other strong support above the grinder. Its large capacity makes filling a sometime affair. To regulate the flow, just crimp the open end. I put a needle valve in the line, because this keeps all the water from flowing out after grinding. A wooden plug would work too.

A telephone shower attachment can be used to deliver a stream or a flood of regular tap water to your hands at the wheel. Just buy one at the local drug store chain, and also pick up a couple of terrycloth towels and rubber bands. Hook up the telephone shower attachment to the faucet and snip the shower end off leaving an open hose. Use the rubber bands to attach terrycloth towel rolls around both arms at the wrists. This will prevent water from walking down your arms into your shoes. The hose end can also be rubber band secured to your wrist and arranged to point out over the pick in hand. Alternatively, the hose can be grasped by one or two fingers and merely held in contact with the pick. The only rule is that the water must actually flood the pick cutting-field and remove the heat before it spoils the temper. The waterbed retailers offer plumbing adapters that will fit to most faucets, and which will deliver water to you at the wheel.

The machinist's solution to the coolant problems is more elegant than a tomato can. There are two types of machine coolant system, the mist sprayer and the flood type. Big-shot experts tell me that research into cooling shows that a fine spray or mist of droplets is most efficient at carrying away heat build-up, so most modern systems use mist-type sprayers and not flood types. The mist cooler is also better suited for the tiny lock pick. The system involved is much less complicated, since it consists of only a small block with an air venturi in to suck the coolant up to the misting nozzle. The block is connected to a shop air supply. The catch is you need a steady supply of compressed air.

The venturi block feeds from the tank via a vinyl tube. Several companies offer a mist coolant system with various capacities. I use the Mist-Coolant brand. The volume per minute of compressed air needed to operate effectively the coolant pump is small, as are the pounds per square inch.

The venturi block works on the same principle that the car carburetor does. Air traveling through the constricted throat of the block creates an area of low pressure, and the coolant is drawn up through a tube and into this area by that vacuum. When the coolant hits that air stream it is atomized and accelerated out through the nozzle. An attached needle screw valve controls the amount of air for a given viscosity of coolant. Plain water feeds fine at almost all pressures, volumes, and knob settings. The Mist-Coolant brand manufacturers also package a coolant concentrate to mix with water and I feel this mixture cools much better than plain water. Of the three families of coolant additives: oils, emulsions, and synthetics, the emulsion is best for this type of work. A mix of 5% oil in water is usual. The industrial supplier who handles the mist units should have a large selection of these coolant mixes to choose from. When mixing up a batch, use only soft or preferably distilled water. Hard water may cause the emulsion to separate during the grinding. If no soft water is available, try a little trisodium phosphate (TSP) in the water before mixing to condition. In the actual mixing, put the correct amount of water in the bucket first and add the oil on top of it or into it. The finished mix should have a uniformly creamy texture. When mixing a new batch of coolant, run some plain water through the system to flush out all the old coolant. It is possible to have coolant spoil and grow bacteria when not in use. A month is the usual shelf life at my shop. Actually, I don't even measure the coolant concentrate closely, since it costs so little per gallon. I usually dump in a sizable gob and grind.

In use, the water coolant is directed to spray onto the steel at all points where it contacts the wheel. A generous flow of coolant will absorb enormous amounts of heat build up and allow continuous grinding, which translates to great time savings.

A pan to catch coolant as it condenses is a must. The amount of coolant you use per unit of time is determined by the amount of air pressure and the amount of throat given the needle valve, but it can add up to a lot over a five minute grinding session. The coolant is gritty and messy with steel particles, and will corrode and stain lots of things in the vicinity.

Any large size metal or plastic container will do if the grinder can fit comfortably inside it. To adapt a plastic dish or storage pan to the grinder, put a wooden plank in the bottom, with a pattern of holes drilled into it to accommodate the rubber feet on the grinder. Mark the positions for these rubber feet by putting layout ink or Magic Marker on the feet and then stamping it onto the wood. Once the grinder is in place, check it for comfortable working clearance, remembering that the wheel will get smaller in time, and also that the steel piece you grind may be as long as a foot. Once you have a position you like, provide cutouts in the metal pan for access to the areas where the hands get close to the grinding wheel face. To guard these edges install a wooden exterior board over the holes, pencil in the location of the pan cutouts, and cut the wood an eighth of an inch INSIDE these lines to provide a comfortable buffer for the wrists. I have a bulk drain hole in the bottom fitted with a rubber stopper. I used a liberal application of silicone RTV caulk to bed the board when mounting the grinder motor in a metal pan.

I do not advise directly recycling the coolant that will collect in the drip pan by laying the mist feed hose directly in the bottom of the pan. Even though the feed hose has a coarse sieve in its end, and a finer mesh could be added, nothing traps all of the particles. In addition, the water component of the coolant will decrease as it is steam-flashed away by the hot metal, while the oil will remain. Eventually an invert emulsion will be formed (see above) which is very bad, so the larger capacity defers the time when this problem crops up. I have a three-gallon plastic tub of coolant mixed up each time and it lasts for about one month of heavy machine time. The first of every month the coolant is replaced with a fresh batch. A teaspoon of dish soap in the pan serves to make the clean up a little easier. When cleaning out the pan use a rag, not paper towels or even cellulose wipers. The small particles of steel can slice right through mere paper and into your hand which is mere flesh and blood. You get enough small cuts from daily operations that you don't need to risk adding to the list. There will be hardened globs of iron oxide particles immediately below the wheel and these can be chipped with a putty knife for removal when they get too mountainous. While I am warming up on free advice here, let me also tell you that I have a regular schedule of tetanus booster shots set up. Pesky metal splinters will cause both minor and serious infections, and they can do even worse. Considering the locksmith's usual working conditions in some of the "ritzier" apartment flats, you could catch anything. Better to inquire with your Doc on any recommendations for keeping up to date on protection. Of course, any cut or "sticker" should be cleaned and dressed with some antiseptic ointment and a Band-Aid. Let me also repeat that the fine mist in the air around the grinder presents a significant health hazard. If inhaled in any quantity, it can lead to shortness of breath and sickness. The coolant additive carries no warning label regarding this, so I have no idea why it is so hazardous, but take it from one who knows from first-hand experience: use a regular respirator when doing any grinding.

Should your mist block get clogged from intake of any foreign material into the feed hose, it shall be disassembled and cleared, using a toothpick, not a metal implement.

Before you put the grinder system into operation for the first time, go over all of the metal surfaces of the grinder with a good grade of moly grease to retard corrosion. This especially applies to the area immediately below and behind the grinding wheel. Large lumps of metal particles that oxidize will form here, and the grease makes them easier to chip out and remove. With moderate use the "mountain" of oxide needs removal once a month, and I usually replace the grinding wheel then also. It is false economy to grind on a wheel even slightly worn down, and can be dangerous as well. When preparing a piece of steel to grind, cut a couple of doughnuts from a cellulose sponge by making circles about two inches in diameter with a slit through the center. These can be slipped onto the steel, and act as drip collars to prevent coolant run-off from trickling down your arm and over the pan sides. The doughnut is jockeyed around in position as the grind progresses. Also, in the less messy department, it's good to have a vinyl or waterproof apron to wear over your usual shop clothes. The mist clouds will wet down everything in the immediate area after a grinding session. Even more crucial, I can't seem to tolerate the mist in the air, and if I breathe just a little in, I suffer for days, so wear a respirator mask.

You may balk at buying an air compressor just to operate a coolant pump. However, I strongly recommend the air system with pump since mist does a far better job of cooling with far less excess runoff. The average locksmith's shop can always use a source of compressed air for cleaning the myriad of metal chips, dusty mortise and cylinder lock cases, drying solvents, and so on.

If you are like me the Reagan-era left old habits. We learned to make do with less then and went to the junkyard. If you would like to cobble together a make-do mist type system, go out and find an old fashioned garden plant sprayer. Look for the trombone-type with the long cylinder, the can at one end, and the push handle. Remove the push handle, cylinder end, and piston. Connect your shop vacuum backwards so it blows out air from the pickup hose, and duct-tape that hose end to the open cylinder. This will provide a continuous, automatic flow of air to atomize whatever coolant you put into the spray bottle. This makeshift version works okay, but is still no substitute for the air compressor driven one. Likewise, using a paint sprayer, air brush, or other atomizer is possible but not as efficient, and probably more hassle in the long haul.

Another possibility is an artist's mouth sprayer. These gizmos are used by artists to spray paint onto canvas. They consist of only a mouth tube to blow through, and a pickup tube to dip into the paint. They can be attached to a couple of vinyl tubes, one going to the vacuum cleaner backblast and the other going to the coolant tank. For large vertical lifts from the coolant tank, or extended grinding sessions, only air pressure from a backward-tubed vacuum cleaner or shop vac will cut it.

For my money there really is no acceptable substitute for a commercial mist coolant attachment. In everyday shop usage you can simply open a supply valve, turn on the grinder motor, and start grinding immediately and continuously. The time savings are well worth the initial cost of setup. If you machine other small metal parts in your shop operations, these can be shaped in a twinkle with such a handy setup! I find that I use a coolant-enhanced grinder just as frequently as a belt-type grinder once it is one-turn-easy to start the flow of coolant.

A couple of paragraphs back, I mentioned the shop belt grinder. Baldor, Kiwi, and other specialty suppliers make these handy machines for abrasive finishing. They take a variety of grit belts, sized anywhere from one to eight inches wide. There is one major advantage to the belt abrasive: it runs much cooler when cutting shim stock into lock picks. I don't know whether this is due to the accelerated wear caused by the sharp edges of the steel "stripping" off grains of abrasive, or to the fact that each square inch of the belt must travel along a 70+" path and be air-cooled before having to make another pass along the hardened steel.

Whatever the reason, it is almost possible to run off a few picks on an abrasive belt with only occasional cooling by immersion in water, if you have such a finisher. I have used both a Baldor and a Kiwi, and I prefer the Baldor. Their machines are closer to the tools produced for jewelers and seem to be more precise for small-parts grinding. Take note that some abrasives belts are made with water soluble binders and are not suitable for any wet grinding at all. Just about all belt finishers also seem to have low-mounted wheel bearings that can be attacked by corrosives like water-only coolant, so experiment on these machines with extreme care. By contrast I have been doing wet/mist grinding on a bench set-up (motor on wood pedestal) for many years and have never had a corrosive bearing failure or even a problem. If you specify resin-bonded belts, they will be waterproof.

Take a tip from eddie and be cool; mist cool that is. If you want to free up lots of time to file finish picks with great brilliance and skill at the bench, tool up with mist coolant and eliminate the biggest time waster in the chain.

Chapter Eight
Finish Filing

Although the rough grind can proceed to within .010″ of the desired contour, finish filing is still necessary to smooth the grind, refine the shape, and tune the flex of the shank. In this chapter eddie talks about the proper use of the file on your lock pick creations.

The pick quickly takes shape at the wheel and it becomes exciting. Standing hunched over the grinding wheel and getting sprayed damp while squinting to see layout lines is like honeymooning at Niagara Falls. It makes a body want to hurry up, dry out, and get on with the good stuff. Because of this impatience factor it is better to rough grind to the layout line and stop there, then clean up and take a coffee break. When you are rested and dried out the pick can be taken to the bench pin and filed the rest of the way. I usually have five or six picks laid out to grind all at once. Then I finish file them hours or days later.

The metal file is actually the best tool for this job, since files offer good control and flexibility at the bench. The file became prevalent in France first, about 1750, and coincidentally the lock began to be more of a high-tech device then as well. Which came first? Files are nothing more than soft metal blanks that have grooves raised on their faces, and are then hardened. The hard teeth are further carbonized (carbon added to the steel) for yet more hardness. So much for the short tour.

As for what type of file to keep and use, you will need three very different types to finish the job. For general rough filing, a single-cut, triangular six- or eight-inch is good. For filing to shoulders you need a pillar profile, double- (sometimes called second-) cut mill with two safe edges, and for finishing off the rough spots left by those files a smooth cut mill file of warding pattern is the best, again in the six- to eight-

inch size. The terms "cut type" and "safe face" need some explanation. A safe edge on a file is a smooth face. Notice in Figure 24 the file will cut on face A but face B is a safe (smooth) edge so it does not cut or distort surface C. When files are diagrammed in a catalog they are shown in end-on view and safe edges are noted. File cuts are classified by how many sets of grooves are cut and to what degree of fineness. They are classified by jewelers as follows:

file cuts	teeth per inch
coarse	14–22
bastard	22–32
second	30–42
smooth	50–68
dead smooth	70–120

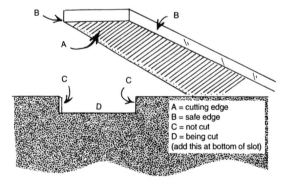

A = cutting edge
B = safe edge
C = not cut
D = being cut
(add this at bottom of slot)

Figure 24
Safe-edge file cutting slot.

The more teeth per inch, the smoother the cut the file makes, and the slower it cuts. The more teeth per inch, the more cleaning is necessary, and boy does that price jump up on those smooth and dead-smooth files. Despite these pain in the ass factors a smooth cut file is a valuable weapon in your arsenal and is really worth hunting up. Its cut does not require any further finishing. The corner hardware is highly unlikely to stock these specialized files, so your best bet is a jewelry makers' or gunsmiths' supply.

Since you'll shell out many bucks for that smooth-cut mill the proper care of a file becomes important. The two rules of file care are that it be kept absolutely oil- and grease-free and that it never be used while clogged with metal particles. This is called pinning and is harmful to both file and work. When I get a new file I put it in a bath of lacquer thinner to remove all traces of shipping preservative. That is the same procedure you can follow for shim steel just before spraying it with layout dye. Anyway, once the file is pulled out of the thinner, swing it around to dry it and then apply a liberal amount of chalk to the teeth. Yes, that's right, chalk. The kind teachers and kids use is just fine, but avoid the really soft stuff. You should fill up the gullets right to the top. Gullets are the troughs between the teeth of the file.

The chalk is what keeps the file from clogging with the metal particles sheared off during use. The metal removed from the pick must go somewhere, and if it gets packed down in the file gullets it reduces the cutting ability of the file. Eventually the file will dull. The chalk sort of immobilizes those particles and holds them until you can brush them out with a file card. The chalk also absorbs any grease left on the work.

Any industrial house will sell you a stiff wire brush with a paddle handle: the file card. In use, the card sweeps the contents of the gullets sideways from the file. The single pointed wire some cards have stored in a sheath on back is a toothpick for tenacious metal particles. Once the file is brushed clean, the chalk is reapplied every time. So buy and use chalk and a file card. If you store all this stuff together it becomes second nature to clean the file frequently. In a half-hour session at the lock pick maker's bench it is wise to card and chalk the file at least ten or fifteen times. How many times do you see someone who never once cleans a file, and wears it out in thirty minutes? If well kept, a file lasts a year or better. One trick to save muscle strain is to hold the file down on the bench pin, not in the air, when carding it. If you grasp both card and chalk in your right hand it will also save time.

The files may have come in plastic or paper sleeves. Either retain these or make sturdy ones out of

heavy cardboard wrapped with tape. On no account allow your files to touch or scrape each other while in the tool drawer or elsewhere, because they will then dull and chip quickly.

As for handles, the supplier carries a variety of plain wood types, and also a plastic one with a hardened screw insert that cuts into the tang of the file as it is screwed on. Some kind of handle is necessary or you will end up with a nasty puncture wound in the wrist from that tang when you slip up. For handles I was taught to cut a five-inch long piece of ¾″ wood dowel, and then burn the file tang literally into the end of the dowel by heating the metal bright cherry red with the torch. It may take a couple of heats to do the job, but it makes a good handle. Take care not to hammer the file in AT ALL since banging on the file's working end will easily chip it. Use only hand pressure and heat to seat it. A dollop of shellac poured in the charred handle recess will seal the wood and make the file stick better. Felt-tip marker on the handle identifies the file if it's sleeved.

Let's proceed to the filing now. To hold the pick for filing you will need a specialized arrangement. My personal filing jig for finishing picks of all types is modified from a stock-pattern jeweler's bench pin. This ingenious device has been used by watchmakers and jewelers for hundreds of years for working small parts, and is close to ideal for lock pick manufacture as well. Over the years I have made three modifications to my pin to suit it better for holding the pick during filing. I will describe the stock pin and then my modifications to it.

The jeweler's bench pin comes in two parts: a metal casting that is slotted at the front to take a wooden piece called a bird's mouth, and a series of wood inserts. This small wooden protrusion is used as a mini-workbench surface when filing, hammering, riveting or sawing jewelry parts. It is very useful because it allows easy access from three sides and lots of angles. The metal casting will have screw holes or a "C" clamp-type screw to fix it to the bench, and also a small metal anvil surface usually used to set rod rivets on. To adapt the wooden pin to lock pick work make the three alterations detailed in Figure 25.

The first alteration is a series of slots that serve two different functions. One is just to hold the pick tightly on edge so it can be filed down. The other function uses both a slot and the top surface of the bench pin. One slot is cut exactly as deep as the desired final width of pick shank. When using this slot during the final width filing, the file will cut down until it begins to bottom on the bench pin. Eventually the file will glide over the wood surface and not cut the shank at all. This gliding action over the smooth straight wooden bench pin will produce a matching smooth cut on the pick shank top surface. These slots are all cut with a jeweler's frame saw of .028" thickness, so that .031" pick steel will be a tight fit. If you cannot locate such a thickness saw, try a thin hacksaw blade.

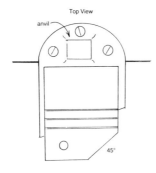

Figure 25
Modified bench pin for a lock pick maker.

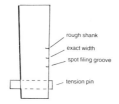

Figure 25a
Side view of pin showing grooves & pins.

Take some time to make these groove cuts and avoid any see-saw effect which will produce a curved bottom cut. Make the final finishing saw strokes absolutely parallel and slow with a tightly strung blade. They should range in depth to take the pick from rough grind to final shank width, and one slot should be very shallow, just enough to permit a toehold for spot filing on the pick shank, and NOT

filing flush with the bench pin. This last slot is little more than a groove. If later working shows one slot is not deep enough (see end of chapter) then carefully cut it deeper. If the fit becomes progressively looser with age and use, try soaking the wooden pin in a mixture of mucilage glue and water to swell the wood. The slots also hold the pick for tip and handle finishing.

The second modification is a 45-degree cut on the corner of the bench pin. This serves as a guide for filing the outside tip and diamond surfaces to the correct angle. A series of shallow cuts into the top right or left edge of the bench pin, or into the front face as well, will be useful in holding the pick for offhand cuts.

The third modification is a tension pin inserted in a hole drilled in the bench pin. It is a friction fit and so can be moved up and down repeatedly and set at different precise heights with a hammer tap. It acts as an all purpose stop and is particularly useful for holding the tension wrench wire when filing flats on same. The wooden surface of the bench pin can also be used to hold the extreme tip of a pick for difficult angle filing jobs. To do this, just press the sharp tip of the lock pick into the surface of the wood and it will lodge there. Once all of the alterations on the bench pin are complete, spray it with a mist of WD-40 and let dry.

To begin finish filing, let's start with a single lifter pick. Initially, you begin with the pick shank top. Use the jig and insert the pick shank top up in the slot and hold the handle with your left hand. A slight away angle keeps the pick bottomed in the slot. There are two critical junctures to avoid filing too deep into. They are the shank-to-handle intersection, and the shank-to-tip intersection.

To safeguard against a slip in those areas, start the file cut short of the pick end by using your thumbnail placed alongside the pick as an initial guide. Go very slowly and make a starting cut deep enough so the file will not jump out past it on the next few strokes. If done properly, it will look like a small diamond or peak on the shank top located just where shank and tip meet. File at a 45-degree angle from the tip at the right to the handle at the left. The critical juncture between shank and handle is only critical if you cut it so deep it weakens. Personally, I like to leave a tiny radius there, and it will not affect the pick performance at all. The only time the pick fails at that point, is when no radius is left there, and the cut strays too far in.

Periodically switching from deeper to shallower slots, the filing should continue cutting the pick shank width until (in the finishing slot) the file slides along the wooden surface of the pin and can't cut the pick steel anymore.

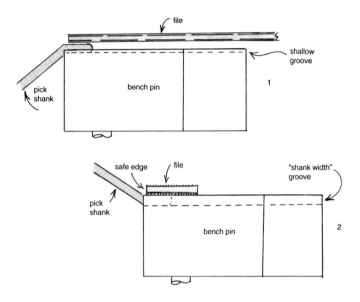

Figure 26
Using groove to file out and inside of pick tip.

The next surface to finish is the outside edge of the pick tip. Place the pick as shown in Figure 26 and hold the file parallel to the side of the bench pin, gauging it by eye. Cut until the surface is fully flat and there is an angle where the tip meets the pick bottom. Now check the angle with your protractor and re-file if necessary. The next surface to file is the inside of the pick tip. There is a trick to make the alignment perfect here. If you place the newly filed flat angle into the shank groove and press the pick tip down into the groove bottom with the file itself, it will pop up and perfectly align. Then you can reapply holding pressure on your left hand. Did you get that all? You hold the pick very lightly in the left hand, press it down into the groove with the file surface gripped in the right hand, just as if you were filing, and then re-grab with the left hand at the correct angle. This procedure can be repeated, even for every file stroke, to ensure proper alignment.

The safe edge of the file is now placed away from where the tip meets the shank, and the tip's inner angle is filed. Filing progresses until the file will no longer cut, making the lifter tip the same width as the pick shank. Now the juncture between the tip inner angle and the shank is worked up. In doing this, always face the file's safe edge into the angle. First cut a little bit on the shank, holding the file over and filing straight down, then shift to the tip and do the same. Eventually, the two surfaces will meet almost in the middle, and form two perfect planes connected by a small radius. Since the tumbler end or tip may find its way into this exact juncture, it must be very clean, with as small a radius as possible. This height-filing jig is not limited to a straight line either. By cutting a slanted or tapered groove in the pin a duplicate taper is produced on the pick. The slant can be very subtle like .005″, or as much as .020-.030″. It appears or rather feels to some operators that a tapered cut on the pick shank works easier in the lock because of the greater solidity afforded. Since the slant matches the type of end-only strain the pick is required to resist, the terminal width can be thus further reduced. In a very confined keyway area, however, where .004″ can be the remaining pin travel required to get to shear line, a taper can cause problems. There is an easy way to test a lock pick that is being filed down to its absolute least workable width. This kink was shown to me by the proverbial old master craftsman.

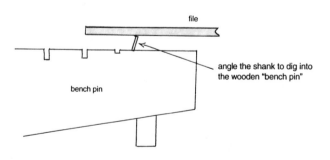

Figure 27
Angle the shank to dig into the wooden "bench pin."

After filing the pick shank down to width in your wooden bench pin filing jig, hold the tool up in one hand and gently flex the shank by pushing down on the working tip against the bench pin. Simulate the normal direction of stress the tumbler would give it. You will probably notice that the shank does not bend in a perfectly smooth curve, but instead seems to take a dogleg down or "break" at some point along its length. Mark that break point with a piece of tape or a china-marking pencil, and replace the pick onto the filing jig. You will have to angle the shank to get it to dig into the surface of the benchpin, as in Figure 27. Start filing the pick shank from your mark down to the working end. Frequently remove and bend test the tool. You will find the point at which the pick seems to start bending will advance steadily along towards the tip as the shank is thinned progressively into a smaller width or taper. Eventually, the shank will describe a fairly smooth curve as it bends. This means you MUST now cut no further or the pick will deform and react poorly in use. You may also find that the difference in width from the widest point to the narrowest is very slight, so little is gained in actual shank-to-pin-end clearance. If the clearance is absolutely critical for your needs, attend to the problem this way. For rammin' around type daily openings leave the tool a consistent width.

To finish-file diamond picks follow the same sequence of cut, but don't tune the shank to minimal width, since that is not critical for that type of pick.

Occasionally the lock pick maker will have a problem like... "the squealer." Not the Jimmy Cagney Bighouse variety, but rather a pick that does not cut smoothly while filing. You remember that pointing the lock pick up into the radius of the grinding wheel will cause it to chatter and catch violently. The squealer is that same principle. If the amount of stock free above the slot exceeds about three times the finished width, roughly speaking, the flex of that free end of metal will cause the pick to squeal as the file alternately grabs and then loses this metal surface. It is actually moving back and forth rapidly. This chattering under the cut reduces the efficiency and is hard on tool, file and nerves. The cure is a more solid hold, obtained by using a deeper cut slot in the bench pin. If you cut four sets of slots in the pin initially, and the deepest is not deep enough, cut it deeper until the job you are doing will not squeal. Then, later, if you need that slot back again, cut a new one. Eventually your tools will be adaptable enough to meet all sorts of tool-finishing problems.

One last point. The jeweler will suspend a cloth or leather bag immediately below the bench pin. This is to catch any precious metal shavings and scrap, which are then recycled. Eddie finds that the bag is just darn useful anyway. Any dropped tool is safely caught (especially chip-prone files) and it is easy to rig up such a bag using some denim jeans material and a coat-hanger wire frame with a formed eye screwed to the bench. In the next chapter eddie will put a handle on that newly filed lock pick.

Previous eddie material talks about "stoning" the pick after rough grinding, so where does this fit in? Do you grind, then stone, and then file, or stone last of all? Do you stone at all?

Stoning a pick with a fine grain stone produces the same smoothness of finish on pick steel as a smooth-cut file. In other words, if you are using a smooth-cut file for finishing, the stone is unnecessary. The smooth-cut file can be *reeeaall* expensive, so I will also talk about stoning.

The stone referred to is the same as a knife-sharpening stone: a natural-cut or synthetically furnace-made equivalent. Stones, like files, come in different grades, sizes, and shapes. Only the smoothest India and Arkansas types work for lock picks. They are sometimes referred to as die stones by industrial suppliers. The Gesswein Co. carries an incredible variety of stones.

Stones should always be used with some form of lubricant oil; either light machine oil (three-in-one) or the equivalent. Eddie recommends Marvel Mystery, if available in your area. Avoid using boiled linseed oil or mineral spirits for lubricant, as they will both cause their own unique problems. Another good lubricant is WD-40, applied frequently. The lubricant floats away steel particles and acts like the chalk does for the file. A new thirsty stone may have to be soaked in oil to break it in.

The actual stoning is simple and done similarly to filing. To find minute imperfections, chatter marks, or waves, use the film director's landscape-shot trick. The three hours just before sunset are called the "golden time" by film photographers because the light comes in almost parallel to the ground, and bounces off the land directly into the eye. The result is that every little wrinkle and depression in the landscape is strongly outlined in shadow and makes a nice visual effect. Ironically eddie's favorite movie is *Wrestling Women vs. the Aztec Mummy*, where this art lighting is a real non-issue.

The grazing light trick (see Figure 28) also locates rough areas on the pick to stone. The same lighting trick is used extensively to read key marks during the impressioning process, so it is worth learning.

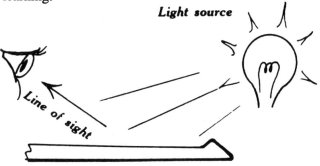

Figure 28
Using grazing light source to examine pick for roughness.

Excessive pressure will make a poor cut, so go slow and press medium firm. From time to time add more oil. Do NOT use your bare finger to check progress or you will get a finger full of tiny sharp-ended steel splinters laced with oil. Use a rag to wipe the pick clean and examine by eye. If you want to do a good job, a magnifying loupe is perfect for this work. They come in all types, mounts and powers. Eddie has used both the eyeglass mount 1.6X power (objects are 1.6 times normal size) and the 3X triplet hand lens. He prefers the latter. To use it, don't hunch over. Sit erect, hold the lens close to your eye, and move the pick in or out to focus. Don't move the lens, move the pick only.

The stone cuts fine and so very slowly, but excessive stoning can still spoil precise contours and sharp points, so take care to avoid this. One area the stone excels at is smoothing contours. Just like dressing the grinding wheel edge to cut a radius on the steel, a stone can be cut with a very hard steel tool like an old worn-out file. This is really good for getting that small radius between pick shank and pick tip just right. Stones may also be purchased in rounds or half-rounds, and these are good for lifter radius smoothing. Treat your stones like sandpaper, or any other replenishable material. If you need a short piece of stone, just go ahead and snap off a piece to use.

Attention must be given to all of the pick surfaces that were ground and filed. All of the surfaces must be accurately deburred in a specific sequence. First, polish the outside diamond, the inside diamond, the shank top, the shank taper, and finally the sides. All of this polishing should be done according to the rule of keeping as much of the stone's surface in contact

with the pick as possible. When stoning the sides of the pick don't then go at right angles to the shank, but lay the stone the entire length of the pick's working shank and stone. The more surface area in contact per unit of time, the flatter and smoother the final surface will be. The shank top can be polished towards the tip using sideways strokes and just a few parallel strokes to finish up with. The bottom of the shank is not usually ground at all, so it should need no polishing.

All polishing need not be strictly parallel with the projected travel of the pick in the lock, since the scratches made by this point are so small they will not seriously impede the process.

As to potential problems, the diamond tip outside and inside is the toughest to do. The first problem is chatter, just like holding the pick higher than perpendicular to the axis of wheel rotation. Always file the diamonds at the proper angle. Secondly, owing to the fineness of the grit it will be impossible to affect any big dimensional change in the steel, but remember the polish can soften some of the hard point on the diamond. As in all things there are two viewpoints on this. One group holds that the hard edge of the angle will produce a greater shocking power as it travels over the tips of the tumblers, and therefore impart more "billiard ball" action to the top tumbler. The other school holds that a rounding there makes the pick run smoother and therefore faster in the lock. You should make a test of your ability to feel minute differences in the performance of a pick in a given lock, so try the tool with a sharp edge first of all, then cut that edge off and see if you notice any difference. I personally favor a sharp diamond. Under no circumstances should the extreme front to bottom edge of the pick be left sharp. This is the part that first enters the lock keyway. It must remain almost sharp so as to lever itself easily under the pin tumbler ends, but you should cut a small radius on it to avoid drag. While it is true that there is an angle cut on the bottom end of the bottom tumbler to facilitate ease of key entry, the sharper the pick (meaning the less flat at the end), the better the pick will enter in a lock with badly worn tumblers. By the way, while I like a sharp diamond, it is partially because of the difficulty I like to feel in jerking the lock; I think that more energy goes into the pins that way, but that may be just my personal fist-action.

After thoroughly polishing the four or six surfaces of the pick, take a minute and cut a 45-degree angle on all of the right angles that border on surfaces you have just polished. This will ensure that no wire edges remain.

The cutting action of the stone will be negligible to nil, but it can slip and you may puncture your hand on the pick, so be cautious and use moderate pressure to stone the pick surfaces. As you use your finely polished lock picks in day-to-day operation, some scratches may develop in their surfaces, and the India stone applied at infrequent intervals will remove these small wear scratches.

Remember to use oil and NEVER stone dry. The light machine oil keeps the stone's surface pores unclogged from steel particles, and lubricates the stone as well. As you polish, it is possible to both see and feel the surface become smoother. By working the pick with oil the cleanest cut possible is guaranteed. If you use oil, leave the stone in the tray for the next cutting session, and cover it with tinfoil or another tray, since it is a fire hazard.

If your picks have been thickness-ground to a smaller clearance at the tip, then stoning of this side-ground surface is essential to good lock picking with that tool.

One exception to normal stoning practice is using the stone to develop a series of cross-hatching scratches on the sides of the pick shank for the purpose of holding oil lubricant. This makes a raking pick work real nice in an older dry-mechanism lock. A final dip and rinse in the oil, drying on a rag, and then degreasing with naphtha or lacquer thinner, and your stoned pick is ready for bob polishing.

Chapter Nine
Polishing Picks

This chapter deals with the last important steps of finishing up your lock pick. There are still some hairline scratches marring the pick even after final filing with a #4 double cut file for those fine outline adjustments. These remaining scratches will not impair the performance of the pick, but in bollixing super-smooth action against the tumblers and in the keyway, they can make the pick relay "false" feedback about the movement of the lock tumblers. This is because the hardened steel edges of the pick cut into the soft brass alloys that the lock tumblers are composed of, and will also "dig" into the keyway surface as well. This abrading action will create some dragging and sticking friction and causes the lock parts to behave as you DON'T want them to: catching on the tool.

This dig-and-hold effect is useful in one place only. The ability to cut selectively into the bottom of a tumbler is a big asset for all types of lifter pick. To exploit this sticky tip effect, the top edge of all lifter picks may be designed especially with a knife-sharp working edge to cause an anchoring of pick tip into tumbler surface.

In all other cases, though, absolute smoothness of action against the tumbler/keyway is desired, especially in a rake or diamond pick and a snake or wiggly/bent riffler. It is also true that I polish a pick (called coloring it in the trade) for looks and beauty. A mirror-shine tool looks so good it gives you an ego boost when you think "I made that." One other point is that a tool carried on your person will be subject to spot rusting as assorted crud sticks to the tool. If it's polished, the tendency to spot up is much reduced.

Here at the shop we use a product called Fabulustre. It is manufactured by the Formax company and it's a stick abrasive formulated for final polishing jobs on a wide variety of metals. It is absolutely the best product I have ever used for that difficult job of steel polishing. Normally eddie doesn't get all mushy over a specific brand-name product, but only Fabulustre seems to work well for pick steels, so ask for it by name. It is usually available from jewelry tool trade suppliers, and a few are listed below.

Allcraft Tool and Supply Company, Inc.
22 West 48th Street
New York, NY 10036

Paul H. Gesswein and Company, Inc.
255 Hancock Avenue
Bridgeport, CT 06605

American Metalcraft, Inc.
4100 Belmont Avenue
Chicago, IL 60641

New Orlean's Jeweler's Supply
206 Charters Street
New Orleans, LA 70130

Ohio Jewelers Supply
1030 Euclid Avenue
Cleveland, OH 44115

Norvell Marcum Company
1609 South Boston
PO Box 2887
Tulsa, OK 74119

Nicholson File Company
667 Waterman Avenue
Providence, RI 02914

Skil-Crafts
305 Virginia Avenue
Joplin, MO 64801

To apply it, use a hard felt bob mounted in a rotary hand tool like your Foredom or Vigor machine, or a bench motor or drill press chuck. The bob should be circular and approximately 1″ diameter with a ¼″ face. A hard felt bob is almost as hard as a soft wood like pine, and in the dimensions you need it should be readily available. Once the cardboard tube is opened up a little, the compound bar end is dipped in kerosene briefly to lubricate the bob face and prevent excessive compound melting. The bar should be applied lightly to the bob while teasing the throttle to keep the speed as low as possible. In this way a good deposit can be built up quickly on a new bob. Once the bob is fully charged, begin polishing on the sides of the pick. The shim steel you have cut your picks from will be matte finish, but the bob will make them reflect soon enough. Starting on the side will also help to break in a new bob easier than attacking the wire thin shank first. The wire shank would just strip off compound. Work from the middle of the pick handle out to the end, moving the tool towards you in short sweeps. The pick is held either on the bench pin or in the air like for grinding. After one half is polished, turn the pick over and do the same half on the other side. Then switch the pick end-for-end and repeat the process. The felt bob will quickly become black from the polishing action against the steel. Charge the bob with more compound at frequent intervals, and remove the excess crud and used felt by raking the bob with a screwdriver blade while running. Notice how the felt bob can even cut the screwdriver. The screwdriver end will even be worn slightly by this raking. Use the same caution and rules when raking as you do when grinding at the bench grinder to prevent the bob from catching and whipping the screwdriver. The possibility of getting badly cut is still just as real at this final stage. Come to think of it, a lock pick is a dangerous tool for its owner all through its working life. The working end (shank and tip) of the pick is polished last, in whatever sequence you find comfortable. The rule is to always polish towards the free end, never into it, just as in grinding. Once you finish polishing, clean the excess compound and steel off with a lacquer thinner rag, and immediately follow it with some fine tool and instrument oil. I prefer the Starrett brand in the yellow bottle. Congratulations are in order, maybe even a celebration: you have just hand-fabricated your first professional class lock pick.

For your information, Fabulustre also does a nice job of coloring brass and nickel silver as well, so if you have fabricated handles, pocket toys, or other tools with these metals, have a go at them with the bob also. The bob should be used from time to time on lock picks in daily use to keep the shine up, and to recolor nickel silver that is carried on the body, since it will develop a tarnish. Remember whenever you clean the pick to reapply a thin film of instrument oil. In particular, don't — repeat — *don't* handle your tools after eating any fruits like apples, oranges, etc. The natural acids in fruit juice will make short work of your polished surface. This can be a neat trick, though. First, lacquer thinner-clean a pick. Then roll a fingerprint onto a fresh apple bite, then onto the exposed steel of the pick, and set it aside on the shelf. In no time at all you will have the ultimate personalized mark, your fingerprint etched onto the tool, and looking kind of pretty! Of course, who would be so bent as to want to steal another man's lock picks? Quite a few. A lock pick set on the sidewalk would be snapped up faster than the proverbial wallet with a crisp twenty inside. Most everybody treats the lock pick with a kind of awe. In Chapter Sixteen, eddie will talk about that some more.

Chapter Ten
Lock Pick Handles

Here's a quote you hear from quasi-experts in the lock pick field from time to time: "Real professionals prefer lock pick tools without handles." In fact, if I hear that line just once more...! Supposedly, that lack of handle enhances the "feel" one receives transmitted from the tumblers to the tool. Contrast this with what the working locksmiths say: most think this is just plain wrong. Not to say that the top-flight locksmith isn't concerned with feel or touch. It's just that the right kind of handle is what's needed. A commercial pick has at least a thin aluminum slab handle, and you get used to it, but it's not the best. Handles are usually lacking altogether on shop-made picks. This isn't usually by choice, but is dictated instead by the difficulties in creating and installing workable handles on the shopmade pick.

The benchmade lock pick cut from .025-.031″ shim stock provides feel all right, altogether too much feel. The near-knife edge of the steel digs uncomfortably into the tips of thumb and index finger during a lock opening, and I believe it really dulls feeling more than enhances it. The common myth for all the youth of my day was the "Jimmy Valentine" safe cracker who could infallibly open combination locks on money vaults or chests simply by feeling when each tumbler clicked into its respective gate. In the popular stories of the day this feel was enhanced by rubbing one's fingertips on some fine sandpaper just prior to an opening. It was a great idea, but I prefer feeling with the skin attached.

That wire edge of the ultra-thin pick handle causes pain, not greater skill at opening. A lock pick that's cut from a jackknife is also just as bad. The problem there is the extreme overweight of the

handle in relation to the delicacy of the task at hand. It is impossible to cultivate a niceness of touch when the total weight of the lock pick is so heavy. Far better too light than too heavy any day, and too fat an edge is preferable to one that's too thin. Serviceable, yet not quite there, is a wrap of electrician's tape. It just does not seem to fill the bill. Both handleless and overweight jackknife lock pick handles have one thing in common; they are make do only.

If you have just finished your pick and are anxious to try it for proper function, that's fine. Go ahead and use it on a couple of locks, but then remember to set aside the time to install a handle and see how much easier it is to use. I will be starting with the easiest types of handle installations, and progressing to the hardest or most complex. (Good plan, eh?) The least difficult handle is called the twist or doubled handle. Normally I do not use this type of handle, but making it will give you some experience in annealing and rehardening the steel, so I include it here. The ability to shape and harden the steel to suit your design aims is a valuable skill. Putting a couple of 20- or 30-degree bends in the handle does much towards aiding leverage feel while making the tool more pleasant to hold.

Before applying any annealing heat to the lock pick tool, remember that the steel has been industrially tempered to its best possible state, and heating the steel will destroy this temper. Of course the temper can be redone, but it is very difficult to match the superior factory heat treatment. That refrain is getting to be like the old "the secretary will disavow any knowledge, Mr. Phelps," I know, but it is important. Making allowances for a heat sink at the working end of the tool will prevent the heat applied for handle bending from traveling down and adversely affecting the working end of the pick.

A heat sink is merely a large mass of metal in good contact with the part of the tool you want to keep cool, or at least cooler than the temperature at which softening occurs. Unfortunately, if you use the largest mass of metal you have (the bench vise), and only use a propane torch for heating, the steel handle will not get very hot, because the heat sink will actually be far too efficient in relation to the amount of heat delivered per unit of time. A more balanced heat sink for a propane torch is the small machinist's clamp, applied about $1/8''$ away from the point you have decided to bend at.

This small machinist's clamp may be in turn mounted in a bench vise with no appreciable added "sinking" effect because the heat is traveling through a bottleneck, namely the small cross-sectioned clamp. A strip of newspaper between the vise and clamp will further enhance this insulation effect, and prevent slippage as well. The trick of inserting newspaper between steel and a clamp works well in other areas of lock pick-making like layout, so try it sometime and you will appreciate it.

Once the clamp is firmly applied the torch can be lit and played on the spot where the twist is to go. The thin shim stock will quickly heat up to a dull red heat and easily bend. To minimize heat loss in bending, I use a piece of wet hardwood with a narrow slit cut into it to bend the steel in the desired direction. A crescent wrench with jaws set to a slit will also work, but grabs heat off rapidly. A bending fork of $1/16''$ steel strip with a hacksawed slit in one end is good for a long-term bench accessory. Mine is screwed to the bench.

Notice that as the heat increases, the familiar "band" of tempering colors appears and travels down the tool handle. This narrow spectrum of colors shows where the heat has untempered the steel. If this band ever shows to have advanced into the working area of the lock pick tool and bypassed your heat sink, then that pick should be discarded. So make darn sure the heat sink is firmly applied and is working effectively so you won't ruin any good tool. If unsure, try your heat sink on a scrap piece of shim steel. It is possible to make a bend too close to the working end of the pick, where the heat will naturally "leak" through to, if the sink is faulty.

The bends shown in Figure 29 are all used on working picks. You should experiment with several degrees of bend and lengths of handle segment between bends, to get the kind that feels comfortable to you.

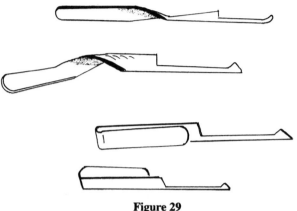

Figure 29
Two styles of twisted steel-only handles.

As you strive to NOT bend the lock pick forward of the handle, it may occur to you suddenly that that may be a good thing. If you hold the lock pick in your hand, it tends to point at a right angle to the arm if you are right handed. This indicates that it is a strain to hold the lock pick so that the end points right at you if you are standing in front of the keyway. It is difficult to assume this posture, which is probably why it is far easier to pick a lock cylinder while held in the hand as you are sitting at the bench. The obvious answer is to bend the handle of the pick at an angle to the pick shank, but this creates new problems.

The big drawback with such a bent pick is that the hand is no longer in a straight line with the pick tip, and if lifting, the lever function has been converted into a twisting, pulling action that is very difficult to control and get feedback from. If the pick begins to resemble your favorite bent slim shim for car knob openings, there will be little relationship between any handle movement and pick tip movement.

It is better if you keep the pencil grip type feel by keeping the pick tip in a straight line with the handle. I recommend that instead of bending the pick, you attach an auxiliary handle to it that will make grasping easier, while still retaining control. The control remains because of the counterweight effect exerted by the handle left in place in line with the pick tip. Later on in this chapter eddie details a foldable clip that doubles as just such a handle.

It is also possible to put a twist or 90-degree axial bend in the handle, and this is very comfortable for certain styles of lock picking. To apply very angular bends like a 90-degree bend, the heat sink is applied as usual, and another clamp is also applied, placed twice as far away from the first one as the shim stock is wide, usually 1″ total. Then the steel is heated to temperature while a twisting motion is simultaneously applied.

There are two points to consider when bending an extreme handle form. One, the bend should be overdone by some few degrees because springback may occur if the working temperature is very low. Two, the radius bends more gradually when worked while the temperature is relatively low. To produce a sharper-angled bend, heat sink the working end, and heat the entire handle very quickly. Then start the bend abruptly, reapplying the torch at frequent intervals. If you apply bending pressure before the steel is very soft, the bend may be more gradual than you want.

If you use a little torch (oxyacetylene) for the bending, the heat sink may almost be dispensed with since it heats so rapidly that the heat has no time to disperse down the handle. It must be quenched rapidly, so keep the bucket at your elbow. The higher heat also allows much sharper bends, almost perfectly compact. I prefer the Smith brand little torch any day, even though it is much more expensive, because it allows infinite control compared to even a #60 tip on a regular torch. Radio Shack also sells a gas brazing torch with both oxygen and flammable gas cylinders (catalog number 64-2165), and this is a good alternative to the expensive Smith brand torch and tanks.

As an alternative to twisting the handle, you can put in fingercuts on your tool, like the handle scallops on a knife blade, but you will probably find they don't make the tool any more comfortable, and are usually in the wrong place for your hand no matter how hard you try to position them accurately. If you want to experiment with these, use a grinding wheel that has been shaped to a small radius with the wheel dressing tool, or cut the scallops in square form and smooth out with a hand file. My number three apprentice's style of work benefits from two half-rounds cut exactly opposite each other about ¾″ away from the beginning of the shank. The small

neck left can be as little as $^3/_{16}$″ in width and still perform well.

If you carry your flat-ended tension wrenches in a pack graded according to size (width) of wrench end, you can start at the narrow end and move up until it catches in the keyway nicely. The added weight is nice also for a tension wrench. A handle pack for these is easily made from a doubled-over aluminum handle strip.

Speaking of aluminum handles, let's talk about those nifty wallet set picks you so coveted when you got a look at your first locksmith's tool catalog. My first set of tools had a handle made out of light aluminum stock in two pieces riveted to both sides of a pick. To duplicate this style of handle you need to layout the hole locations on the pick steel, anneal and drill holes, then transfer hole locations to aluminum or brass handle scales and drill these, finally riveting the assembly together. It is also easier to do spot annealing if the places are clearly marked.

If you are using a carbide scriber to make the layout lines, annealing the steel prior to layout is not necessary, but annealing IS necessary prior to punching and drilling a hole in the steel. So, if you can accurately spot anneal, then construct the layout and drill, so much the better.

We will now spot anneal the handle, but don't get out your torch just yet. It is also possible to heat up just a tiny spot where you want the hole to go, using a technique called spin annealing. A spin anneal involves minimal heat bleed and therefore is much more accurate. The tool to do that with is a heat-treated (and it absolutely must be heat-treated) prick punch. Carefully grind off the point and finish a flat spot on the end instead. Chuck this tool into the drill press and set the belt for the highest rpm possible. The spot for annealing can be marked with a light carbide scriber mark, or a couple of fences set up on the press table will align the handle properly. The handle must also be firmly clamped onto a block of wood to prevent disaster if the punch catches and holds the handle. It could whip around and end up as a flying sharp-pointed missile. A simple jig with a pin set into the wood on each of three sides of the pick handle will both position and hold. Bring the heat-treated flattened point of the punch down onto the handle and begin to bear down on the drill press handle. The pressure exerted will produce a lot of friction, and that friction in turn produces heat.

Enough heat will be generated to run the temper colors on the steel handle. This means the temper on the pick steel has been removed at that spot, while the heat-treated punch remains unharmed. The handle can now be left to slowly cool off, or lightly water-spritzed to cool it quickly.

Inspection of the spot will show the familiar blue/peacock temper colors. This area can now be subjected to a layout, prick-punched and drilled for the insertion of a rivet. It will still be hard but drillable. If you have trouble with this technique, it's usually because the spin speed isn't high enough. If your drill won't do this, stick with a torch anneal.

Use a light coat of layout dye on the correct side of the pick and a small patch on the backside. The object is to scribe a line exactly midway on the pick. To do that, use a pair of dividers set by trial and error on the wrong side patch until they scribe down the exact middle of the pick stock. The first try will leave a little space between the two lines as you scribe from both sides. Set the dividers to scribe a line halfway through this small space and try again. Observe closely that you don't overlap the dividers and start scribing lines past center. Once set perfectly, you can mark the layout line on the good side. If the pick stock is exactly ½″ you can set the divider to ¼″ by "clicking" the two tines or legs. Seat one point of the divider into the etched line on a machinist's rule, and then adjust the divider until the second point falls precisely into the other etched line at the length you desire. By alternately rocking the points of the divider in and out of the two etched lines, the feel will tell you how precisely the divider is set. Next, reset the gauge to the first hole dimension from the end of the pick, and by holding the gauge on the end of the stock the first hole can be located as in Figure 30. Now prick-punch the line intersections and set your dividers for the distance between two rivets. I usually make this dimension 2½″ by habit, but any reasonable spacing is just fine. The only pitfall is putting the second hole too near the front and allowing the spot anneal to creep into the working shank area of the pick. This would be fatal, so avoid it. Using the center as a pivot, arc the divider over the centerline and prick-punch this for the second hole. The advantage to layout sequencing like this is that you now know

exactly how far apart the two rivet or other fastener holes are. Once these holes are drilled, both handle blanks can be clamped to the underside of the steel and drilled as one. To make the aluminum or brass handle blanks, just use the finished pick as a tracing template and scribe the handle shape onto the raw material, or alternatively use layout dye on the handle blank. The stopping place for the handle should be carried no farther forward than where the pick starts to taper from a full handle width. For a nice radius, reverse the handle and trace the round back at the front also. If an aluminum handle is applied it can be marked. I use a die stamp set for this, and they are inexpensive at the industrial tool outlet type places. Assemble your code like "2 X 35" and clamp the stamps together very loosely, then stamp along the line. You may also clamp a toolmaker's clamp to the handle material and align the first stamp to it. Then keep the first stamp in the impression it just made and align the second stamp to it and the clamp. Lightly stamp, remove the first stamp and heavily stamp the second, then continue on down the line.

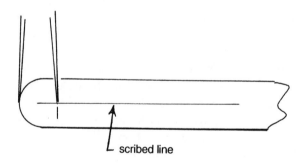

Figure 30
Scribing handle rivet holes equal distance from sides & end.

Aluminum is certainly not as pretty nor as heavy as brass. The added weight of the latter is a big advantage for the lock pick artist "fist." The disadvantage of brass is that it tarnishes easily, especially if carried in your pocket-pick wallet. A good alternative is nickel silver, a common jeweler's alloy which cuts easily. I recommend thickness of 8-10 gauge. The nickel silver handle material in 8 or 10 gauge will come in a large sheet from the rolling mill, and as such it is too heavy to easily rough grind to shape on a wheel. The proper way to do it is with a jeweler's saw.

The venerable jeweler's saw has been around for hundreds of years. It's still the quickest way to produce tiny intricate shapes in thin sheet metals. Jewelers, watch makers, instrument makers, and even lock pick specialists rely on it. The better made jeweler's saw comes with an adjustable end piece with a clamp screw, and a fixed clamp with the handle attached as well. The variety of saw blades available goes from 4/0 up to 10. Different manufacturers have their own numbering systems, so check with your supplier, or even better, buy right at the supplier. The tighter the turning radius of the blade required by the pattern, the smaller the blade that should be selected. For straight cuts, the largest available blade size is fine, and makes the work easier. Most handle-pattern designs will have a lot of straight cuts, so get the larger sizes for sure. They can be found in dozen lots, and even in gross lots as well. Notice that the blade has no attachment points. It is merely clamped into the screw anvils. The teeth can be very tiny, so use your touch to orient the blade correctly. Pinch both blade sides and run your two fingers over the blade, and in one direction one finger will catch on the teeth. This is how to determine which is the outside, and which is the correct cutting direction. The teeth are put in to cut facing out, and to cut on the down stroke, which is against the "V" mouth you will be cutting on. The moveable half of the saw frame should be adjusted so that the blade clamped in the handle end comes up to only one-half of the width of the moveable clamp. To tension and clamp the blade, rest the moveable end against the edge of the workbench, and push the flexible frame in with your stomach. Push in until the blade bottoms in the clamp, then tighten it. The blade should make a singing sound when it is plucked with the finger. A loose blade breaks too easily, and an overly tight one breaks also, but you will learn to judge this by feel. To save a lot of sawing time and ensure that both handle halves are of exactly the same contour, the two blanks can be tack soldered together and sawed as one piece. If you do this, first make the two or three solder joints at the edges where the waste pieces will probably come. After picking the handle assembly, do the layout on one piece only. The saw is held with the handle down, and the blade perpendicular to the piece of work. Excessive side bending of the blade, or twisting in the kerf, will only break the blade, which is brittle to begin with, and only gets more brittle with use. You can use some spit or beeswax on the blade to act as a

lubricant, if you make a mental note to degrease the wax from the sawed-out work before any final soldering operations. To make the initial entry with the blade, hold your fingernail close to the work layout line, and using it as a guide pull the blade up (non-cutting direction) several times lightly against the work, rubbing in a small slot. Once the slot is established, begin sawing in earnest, perpendicular with the work. Very little pressure is required to hold the work against sawing pressure, and any clamp will have to be moved frequently for curves. A clamp may also mar the work if not padded. Despite this, I do use a machinist's clamp with a single layer of newspaper rubber cemented to the jaws. This is very useful for the long straight-edge cuts made so frequently. Curves in the design are negotiated by moving the work piece, and keeping the blade's motion forward and straight. The initial curve is done by moving the blade in the same spot and rotating the work. This cuts a starting "hole." If you are doing handle designs that call for a lot of curves, it will pay you in time saved to have two saw frames, one loaded with a saw blade just for the curves. The price of a good saw frame is negligible, compared to the continual hassle of mounting and remounting blades. Be advised that your first sawing will be jerky and uncertain, and you may break quite a few blades before you get the hang of it. It is best to start on straight lines for that reason, and to saw the more difficult curves later on. With very long lines you may exceed the width of your frame. Some frames allow you to turn the blade 90 degrees, but anyone can duplicate this same action, just by twisting the blade at both ends. Apply a quick firm twist with a pair of small needle nose pliers to both ends. This blade revolving allows you to cut to any length.

For a nice finish leave the handle blanks slightly oversize and file or belt-grind them to fit after rivets have been installed in them. A grinding wheel will pick up aluminum/brass particles and clog up, so use a crummy mill file for final finish and chalk it before use. Clean it with a file card after use. Alternative handle materials also include coin silver, hard red vulcanized fiber sheet, and wood at least $1/16"$ thick. Of special note are the countertop laminates. They have various trade names: Wilson Art and Formica are the best-known. They come in a virtually unlimited variety of colors and patterns. One company has recently re-released the cool countertop patterns of the 50s. Cut-offs or special order sheets come in any size you would need for pick handles. To cut and shape it any power or hand saw with lots of teeth per inch or lots of speed will work. It may even be formed with abrasive belt sanders. To do a lot of handles at one sitting is more economical of your set-up time. One particular advantage of the plastic laminate is its strength. That strength makes it possible to form the handle much larger than the steel pick handle, because it will hold up to strong gripping pressure without any deformation. If you design handles from plastic laminate, remember that the laminate may protrude different amounts of each side beyond where the metal handle leaves off. A wider handle with asymmetrical sides like in Figure 31 actually feels quite nice, and allows finger pockets in the right places to exert some torsional stress on the pick if needed.

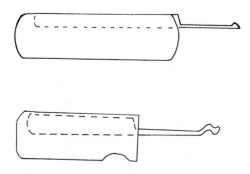

Figure 31
*Oversized plastic laminate handles
with phantom view of pick steel.*

Before you cut a handle, make a cardboard pattern to experiment with. The custom knifemakers use this trick to good advantage and it works well. A piece of thick cardboard should be folded in half and then folded around a pick handle, taped in place, and cut to the approximate size and shape you are looking for. If the feel is not good, cut a little or try another handle until your design settles into a groove. Once you have a working cardboard pattern, the handle may be traced onto paper pattern sheets or directly onto the Formica if it is light colored. If you find one or two types of handle work well for you, it is worth producing a router master mask. Cut out exact size templates of the handle in ¼″ plywood, and attach these to a larger baseplate

of plywood using glue and light nails. Note that you must leave room for the router bit to work. See Figure 32. This piece can be clamped or permanently secured to the workbench. To use this mask, lay a sheet of the desired Formica cut large enough to cover the mask to it's perimeter, and clamp at the extreme edges, where cutting will not occur and the router base will not jam in. Find a hollow spot by doing the hidden passageway tap, and plunge the router in. Alternatively, you can drill a starting hole and position it accordingly. The hole is also necessary if your router has a roller pilot and is not designed for any plunge cutting.

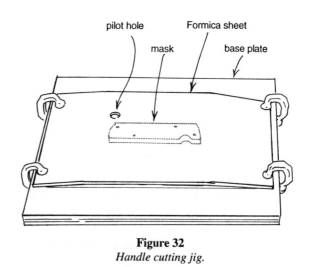

Figure 32
Handle cutting jig.

Plastics can of course be applied with the contact cement formulated to hold them to wood countertops, but riveting will stay forever, even with extreme pick handle flexing. If you use glue, remember to remove all traces of grease and oil from the pick.

If you color-code pick noses so all green handle picks are lifters, all red handles are diamond rifflers, all yellow are ball rifflers, and so on, it will look very professional on the job. To attract less attention, matte black is also available. Coding can also be done by cutting a series of grooves in the pick, with a triangular file, or drilling dimples in. This Braille-type system is not only for night use, but anytime you do not want to glance away from the job at hand.

Another useful plastic material is the stuff they router-cut those custom signage plates out of. You see 'em just about everywhere in corporate America today. This can be had in sizes to match most usual pick handle sizes, and it can be cut with a jeweler's saw, or shaped on the belt sander. As an added feature, any kind of marking code you designate can be inscribed into the handle prior to its being worked into shape. After all, that's what the signage people do. Not just names and numbers but any code you devise, and it will be decipherable in total darkness with a little practice, since it is cut into the surface. This plastic is difficult to glue and absolutely must be riveted. Ask the company if they have trashed signs with misspelled names or extras for guys like Edsel or Milkin. The price could be right. They also come in an assortment of colors.

You can even make handles quickly out of such easy material as duct or electrician's tape. As you wrap this, spacers like wood matchsticks or a split dowel can be inserted to bulk up the handle. The truth is they will slip and turn soggy after hard use, and should be avoided on a professional tool. It is not the hallmark of a patient locksmith to take any easy or quick way out when building a tool to last a lifetime. A very handsome-appearing handle can be made by putting two .020″ brass or fiber scales or blanks on, and two pieces of an exotic hardwood over these, just like a custom-produced folding knife. Nickel silver rivets will look better on a tool treated like this as well. The wood can be tapered towards all sides with sandpaper after riveting. Finish a handle like this by soaking it in linseed oil for ten minutes, then wiping dry. As an alternative finish, fill a jar deeper than the pick handle is long with a quick-drying varnish or wood lacquer, and suspend the handle in the liquid. Now very slowly draw out the handle, either by hand or by wrapping thread around a paperclip windlass or some other jury rig. The slow remove will evenly coat the handle with no drips or sags. Very beautiful. Any wood you use can be colored with felt-tip marker. Some types leave a beautiful color that will not be greatly affected by a lacquer finish. It is also possible to soak the wood in colors made up from Rit cloth dye.

Rit brand (and others) cloth dye is available at most fabric stores, even grocery stores. It is meant to be diluted in water, but you can use wood alcohol instead to dissolve it. There will be some solid residue if you do this, and it can be filtered off. The strong color dye this makes will quickly saturate wood, especially the lighter colored varieties such as oak and maple, and will also dry rapidly. Remember: wood alcohol is flammable and toxic. DO NOT HEAT THIS MIXTURE, and don't breathe the fumes. Do this outdoors. Soak for about ten minutes, remove and dry, and then finish with lacquer or varnish. Some types of finish may attack the dye, so experiment.

Any handle material you choose should not be expected to remain on the steel if it is only epoxy glued to the pick. The fault is not with the glue, but with the steel. Since it flexes easily, the bond between any handle material and the steel will eventually weaken and give way. In all cases a rivet of some kind should be used instead. The riveting technique using nickel silver wire bits is very easy and forms the most secure bond. Spot anneal the steel handle to allow drilling. Mark the wire you choose for the rivet stock and make the hole same size or larger by no more than .003″. If you have a set of number drills, you can often match exactly the diameter of commonly available sizes of nickel silver rod or wire. Scribe a centerline on the pick and space your holes as required on it. It is my custom to retain the divider setting used for the center line, and, holding it on the finished end of the pick, scribe the first hole location. That hole can then be center punched. The divider can now be reset for any other desired rivet spacing, and the second hole location scribed, registering the divider in the first center punched hole. The rivet wire should protrude about $^1/_{32}$″, and no more, above the finished surface on both sides. Insert the wire to check for height, and use a jeweler's saw to mark for the cut line. Remove the wire and complete the cut with saw on the bench pin. The rivet is inserted into the hole or handle pack and oiled slightly. The pin must be a close fit. If it is very sloppy, the situation may be saved by removing the pin and laying it on an anvil surface. By striking the rivet pin on the side softly with a hammer to form a flat, it will fit better. This deformation of round theoretically makes it wedge into the larger hole. If not, repeat until it is acceptably tight. A cross-peen hammer is used to lightly impress a series of cross-cuts into each rivet end. The rivet is turned 180 degrees for another set of hammer strokes until the crosses are both secure enough to retain the rivet and handle parts. Once the cross-peening is done, the rivet is mushroomed against a flat anvil or steel block surface, domed with a doming punch and hammer, or simply planished down flat with the other end of the cross-peen hammer. Do NOT use either face of your cross-peen hammer to drive a doming punch; use a regular bench hammer instead. If the rivet was too long and the end protruded too much above the surface of the handle, the end will mushroom and then crack along its edge margin. You may possibly even lose part of the head. If you crack a rivet, replace it altogether. If you sense a sudden increase in resistance or rebound from the riveting hammer, a crack is imminent. If so, stop with the hammer and file a little metal off the rivet top, and no crack will develop. It only takes a slight amount of flare in the rivet to hold the tool handle on dependably for years of hard use. Half the battle is knowing when to STOP. If you have done a fair amount of cross peening or hammering on the rivet, it may work-harden. When the metal work hardens it becomes difficult to cut it with the file. It behaves as if it was hardened by heating and quenching. In fact, it is hard, and the way to resoften it so the file will dress it down easily is to anneal it with the torch. Try to do this quickly or you will risk damaging the pick steel by overheating. Once cooled it can again be filed easily.

I have been asked if manufactured (called mechanical) rivets aren't better, but I have just never tried them. To me, the nickel silver rivets are preferable, since they can be produced to match the exact thickness of handle pack required. Also, an inexpensive stick of wire will last a long time, and they take an excellent polish when the pick is finished on the wheel. Most importantly, if the handle hole is beveled the plain rivet can be pulled down flush with the handle and polished to almost disappear. Any sharp edge on the handle only distracts me from the delicate job of using the pick, and handles are supposed to help, not annoy.

For all of the single picks I carry I make a riveted pocket clip, as shown in Figure 33. This clip can be extended straight back for use, giving you the unique advantage of a pick handle almost a foot long. This extra length translates into more inertial mass, and makes lifter crowbar picking just that much easier. If you feel the tool is over-balanced this way, set the clip to the "O" clock position of your choice, or modify clip length to make the handle feel comfortable. That's the unique advantage of making your own tools.

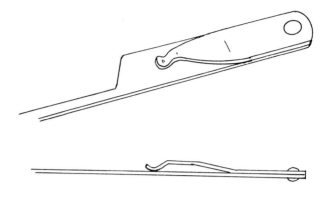

Figure 33
Lock pick handle with riveted pocket clip.

Let me pause here and make a point. Do you know one of the REAL advantages to being able to make your own picks and tools? I produced an absolutely beautiful pick a couple of years ago. It had a high polish, smooth contour lines, worked very well in my toughest test locks, and had a graceful feel as well. I carried it for ten months or so, but one day I plain, stone, lost it. Now, if it had been purchased it would have been expensive, difficult, maybe even impossible to replace, if the supplier was out of business. Instead, I pulled a tracing template and working drawings from the files and got busy again. In less than six hours I had a near duplicate of that missing lock pick. The missing lock pick, by the way, turned up later in a folded grocery bag, and I still have no clue how it came to be there, but I do have a matched set now. A buddy of mine used to have a vibrating-type lock aid tool with a matching belt-mount battery pack. He broke a part and couldn't use the tool again because the manufacturer was long gone. The moral is: tools you make can be replaced or, even better, made better.

Back to the lock pick with attached pocket clip. The clip itself is a smaller piece of steel shim stock. Thickness can be from .020 to .031″ for best results. After cutting it to a rough length, anneal the entire piece of clip with the torch, then coat the entire piece with layout dye and draw a profile on it like the one in Figure 33 or one more to your tastes. At the soft (annealed) end of the lock pick center a rivet hole punch mark and drill it for the size of wire used to rivet. For this rivet, which will also act as a swivel, use $1/8$″ nickel silver wire for the necessary strength. Now clamp the clip over the pick and drill through the first hole into the clip. The clip must be curved to act as a pocket clip. Grip the rivet end with a machinist's clamp and make a 10-degree downward bend in the steel. Notice that the steel is still very difficult to bend even though it is soft. Steel does not get like paper during annealing, just a little softer. Now work the clip over a rod held in a bench vise or over the bench edge to get a curve in the clip. At the very end of the clip make a reverse bend to allow cloth to slide under. Now remove the layout dye and emery polish the clip along its entire length. Place the clip on a pumice pan or preferably a pair of firebricks, set at right angles, set out the motor oil, and spark the torch. Heat the clip until it is non-magnetic, and quench it in the motor oil. Repolish the clip with emery cloth, and do the final temper to peacock or blue. It MUST be done very slowly, and the critical area is the major curve and flat spot where the rivet comes, since stress is greatest in these areas. After tempering, polish on the wheel, and keep the heat down. It is possible to untemper the pick just from the friction heat created by the polishing wheel. Use a can of water to cool the tool.

I have even done a couple of handles in fiberglass, and I think it shows great promise, so I will explain the technique. Fiberglass spa or shower shells are composed of a sandwich. First is a layer of epoxy plastic or hardened resin, then a layer of resin impregnating glass fiber cloth or matting, and finally a final coat of clear resin again. The glass adds bulk and tensile strength, and the resin adds compressive strength and smoothness, as well as tying the whole pack together. The commercial kits put out by auto-body companies to do fiberglass repairs on metal car bodies can provide you with an inexpensive one-shot supply for fiberglass and resins. Since there is a mix or pot life factor, it pays to do a few handles at the same time. Once the initial coat is mixed and the steel degreased, it can be troweled on, popsicle-sticked on, or even dipped and the excess scraped back into the can. The initial resin dip should be wrapped with fiberglass matting about a minute after, and then saturated another minute later. The resin must be worked into all the nooks and crevices of the fiberglass matte for the proper strength. The final coat is applied like the base coat, and the whole pack is wrapped in sandwich wrap or heavy polyethylene sheeting. This holds the shape of the free-form unmolded

fiberglass, and provides a fairly smooth finish as well. The cure time of the resin can be significantly decreased by heating the metal end of the pick with a candle or alcohol lamp. Not enough to glitch the temper or even make the resin bubble, but it will lower cure times. The fiberglass resin actually cures by exposure to heat, and the heat comes from a chemical reaction triggered by adding the catalyst (hardener) to the resin. The candle just helps things along a bit, and even prevents the reaction from going slower than normal because of the heat conducting properties of the steel pick AWAY from the resin. Once the resin is cured, the handle may be shaped on a disc sander wheel or belt sander. If you sand at all, be sure to take the precaution of wearing adequate breathing protection. It is said that inhaling fiberglass dust is VERY hazardous to your lungs.

If you wish to attempt to make a form-fitting handle, just grabbing the plastic-sheet envelope in your mitt and letting the epoxy cure like that will do the trick. A perfect form-fitting handle never seems to be really comfortable except in one precise position, and the real problem is that it is very difficult to attempt lock picking with a single hand position. It is kind of like the finger-scallop cuts thing. You should try the form fit thing though, because a little post-processing will even up the problems. Once the fiberglass has cured and you have used the pick for a few openings, make a note of the handle parts that seem to be in the way. These can easily be altered, smoothed down further, or even removed outright with a belt sander. Don't waste a fine metal file on the gummy resin. It seems as if, all things being equal, an amorphous blob handle is better.

Annealing the steel blanks to make them softer allows you to drill the handle later for a wire rivet, or screw and nut. This will allow you to make a combination pack of pick tools, or just corral single tools by hanging them together. If your working style involves changing tools frequently, this isn't for you. The advantage a pack offers is the increased handle weight and levering action you can exert when the picks are spread out at right angles. Like most picking techniques, some love it and some hate it. I suspect the pack-of-picks craze started with people cutting lock picks out of those little automobile spark plug gap sets. They have the minimum kind of steel in them, although the quality is low-carbon, but they are too short for a good working tool. If you want a secret agent set, use your own steel and make such a set.

If you want both tools to have flush edges when riveted together, clamp the next tool in a vise with the drilled first one, the drilled one on top, and anneal the next handle using the hole as a guide, or use the wood with pins for fences. Once the second handle is heated up, the hole can immediately be drilled through it without waiting for it to cool. Alternatively, a stack of three tools can be annealed and drilled in one operation. The proper drill press setup to use is shown in Figure 34. The toolmakers clamp keeps the handles aligned throughout the process.

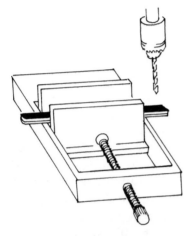

Figure 34
Vise used to safely drill rivet holes in pick handle.

Just because you have a hole in the handle doesn't mean all picks will have an identical contour. It is easy to build a grinding jig to true up the radius of the tool. Drill a hole two- or three-thousandths smaller than the hole size into a scrap of steel, and insert a pin the same size as the pick-handle hole into the steel. You may have to heat up the steel piece to get a good fit. This jig can now be used by putting the pick hole over this pin, and rotating it in contact with the grinding wheel. The radius resulting will be very uniform.

The jewelers' trade suppliers sell an oxygen/-propane torch under the trade name "Little Torch," and I find it is just great for this kind of spot annealing. In operation, you open one valve and light the propane first, adjusting for a fairly large brush-type flame, then slowly feed oxygen from the second valve, and the flame narrows to a small, intensely hot pinprick of light. This little flame will heat and anneal a tiny spot on your picks anywhere you want, and right bang now. Since the flame is so hot, it flows a lot of heat in rapidly and does the job before the metal conduction spread even starts. Cool this with an air blast. It really is a nifty tool.

There's always a catch: they cost over $130 at major city suppliers, less from mail-order. The small tanks they come with don't last at all. For a serious locksmith, the only way is to invest in a complete oxyacetylene welding outfit: tanks, cart, regulators, torch and tips. The small female pipe thread fittings that come with the little torch may be attached to quick-change couplers. The other half of the coupler is in turn attached to the regular torch hose. This allows you to shift from small to large torch safely and quickly. The standard size tanks will last a good, long time just driving the little torch, and the money saved will soon pay back the outlay costs. A further advantage to owning a torch like this is you can also do silver soldering on broken lock parts that are unobtainable.

This covers most of the handle-forming techniques eddie uses. It is very important that all of your working tools have some type of handle, because this will mark you as a professional lock pick tool maker. If you use handleless picks you will never get top efficiency in picking skills.

Chapter Eleven
Tension Wrenches

Tension wrench design theory is covered in the chapter on the theory of lock pick design, so I will deal only with the actual making of these wrenches here.

There are some easy (meaning quick) approaches to making these tools, and also more time-consuming methods. Eddie once saw a guy make a tension wrench from a piece of brass tube and a hunk of music wire in about two minutes. Here's how. Find the approximate middle of the wire, and bend it into a sharp "V" shape. Shove the bent middle into the brass tube and leave two inches sticking out. Swedge (slam) the tube around the wire with a hammer tap. Now grab both ends of the wire with a pair of pliers and bend them 90 degrees. Finally cut the free wire ends to the same length, about $^{1}/_{8}''$ from the bend. This is a double-ended wrench whose ends are inserted into a keyway top and bottom. Bend the wire to give them a slight outward spread. This works like a charm in double-bitted disc or wafer locks where a regular wrench would be pulled out by the pick action. You may also try it in regular pin openings as well. As my good friend Dave says, "Who's going to stop you?" By the way, for a professional version of this same double end tension wrench, read on.

On to the in-depth methods. The standard steel shim stock you cut your picks out from can also be cut into tension wrenches. Figure 35 shows a roughed-out lock pick in the process of being converted into an "L"-shaped tension wrench. The width of the end can be adjusted as shown to match a keyway very closely, as long as you don't cut too much off.

The handle on such a tool may occasionally cause trouble if used on a near-flush mounted lock. In such cases, the fat handle will drag on the door surface. There are a number of ways to get around that. The easiest is to cut the working tip at a slight angle to the handle as shown in Figure 36. This usually provides the needed clearance. If the shank of the tension wrench is long enough and the steel is thin enough, it can be cold-bent in a slight upward twist which will also serve to offset the wrench handle from its right-angle orientation to the tip.

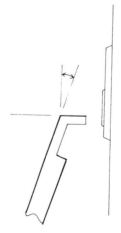

Figure 36
*Note splayed tension wrench
provides handle clearance.*

Figure 35
*Rough pick blank converted to
flat style tension wrench.*

The width of the working handle should not be left at a full ½". It is much better to cut it down further to a ¼" or even less. In fact, you should make an experiment to determine the style of wrench grip that you customarily use. This information will help you in tool design.

Simply put, you are going to mark a tension-wrench shank with Vaseline jelly and then use it to do a few openings. The printed area will indicate how far up or down you hold the wrench and how much area is actually in contact with your fingers. ATM and other keypad codes are often read using the same dodge. It's something a security pro should know about. Close observation also tells the story. Based on this information, length of wrench (for instance) can be determined.

Sequence for scribing lines for layout.
Scribe #1 first, and so on.

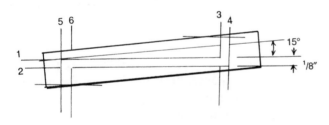

Figure 37
Layout for double-end wrench in ½ stock.

The logical extension of such a wrench is the double-ended whirligig wrench. This type is cut from a layout scribed in layout dye sprayed on the wrench blank. In Figure 37 you will see the usual type of layout. Notice that the wrench lines are actually at angles to the existing edges of the steel. The easiest sequence of line scribing is indicated in Figure 37. The long angle lines are executed first, at a shank width that you are comfortable with. The wider the width the more rigidity this wrench has. For a starting point try a width of ⅛". If you find this too loose for your style, then expand it accordingly. To vary the spacing of the first two lines, and hence the shank width, execute one first and then set your divider points using an engraved rule to the inch fraction you want. Use the scriber to locate a starting point for the

second line, and then align the protractor and execute the second line. The angle protractor is set to an angle of 15 degrees. For a longer wrench use less angle.

To scribe the nose layout lines shift the protractor 90 degrees (keep the setting locked in and twist the entire protractor so a different side contacts the steel shim stock edge), and scribe away. Once all the lines are done, grind and finish in the usual way.

To pack more punch than the double "ell," a tee, a fat H, or whatever other contour seems useful to you, can be laid out. However, with a grinding wheel that is sharp and unglazed and mist coolant flowing freely it will not take long to rough out a couple of double-end wrenches from stock of .025" or better thickness.

Because of that same limited thickness this wrench style will not have tightly fitting tips, but will instead combine springy shanks with loose-fitting tips that rotationally cam or wedge in at an angle to the keyway. This is, of course, one position of wrench type, and it asks the question: "Which came first, the stock available or the wrench design?" You are aware that traditionally tight-nose wrenches have round shanks and loose wedgie-nose kinds have the flat .010-.040" shank. Let's move on to the second wrench and stock type.

The second possibility for stock steel is blank drill rod. This is also from the industrial supplier of shim stock. As you know, drills themselves come in fractional sizes ranging from ¹/₃₂" to ½" in 64th-inch increments. You may not be aware that drills also come in a progression of other sizes termed letter and number drills. The numbers sizes run from 1-60, the decimal on this series is from .009 to .230. The number series drills run A-Z and the decimal sizes there are .234 to .413. These additional series of drills are valuable to the lock pick technician because they allow you to size holes very closely to pins and rivets due to the smaller steps between sizes. Number and letter drill sets come from the industrial suppliers. Drill rod blanks come in the very same decimal increments, usually in three foot lengths. For most wrenches the number sizes from # 25 to # 45 will serve very well.

The rod comes in two steel types, water-hardening and oil-hardening. The water-hardening is the easier to work with and temper, although both are high-carbon steel. The actual wrench is ground with opposing flats that are either parallel or taper gradually thinner to the nose tip. With correctly tapered flats this design is very tight fitting, and the initial diameter of the rod ensures that it will be very rigid at the shank as well, despite the degree of temper.

Notice again that these two types of steel each produce a tool that conforms to each of the two schools of thought. The shim stock makes a loose fit springy wrench, and the drill rod makes a wedge fit rigid shank. Further, each tool corresponds to a selection of pick and a type of lock opening technique. Since the 20s or so, this matching of plug wrench and pick type has prevailed.

What would happen, you ask, if a tight tip were matched with a springy shank? As you know, a tight-fit wrench is not commercially available and so must be shop-made. The tools which are made are very rigid, so the tight-nose springy-shank plug wrench hardly ever comes up. I tried thinning a rod shank by face-grinding, and I will tell you the results are very interesting. I thought initially that a springy shank response would cancel out any feedback feeling that the tight-fitting tip wrench usually produces in operation. A tight tip with a shank that is somewhat flexible is quite nice. The key here is the "somewhat." Too limp a spring is no good at all, too rigid gives no better feel or fist. In between I find that for my style it is the IDEAL wrench. Later in this chapter I give instructions on building this wrench type. I also show how to adjust it to its peak performance.

A further redeeming value is that it prevents accidental total loss of twist because of its built-in reserve of twist so to speak. Even if the hand slips, there is still some twist built-in, where with a rigid shank this is fatal.

One other point worth mentioning before we dismiss, is that moderately tight-fitting wrench noses will never slip around or, even worse, kick out during a long period of picking. The big advantage to a wedge-nose plug wrench is that you don't need to be so painfully careful about accidentally knocking the plug wrench free and causing a pin "zipper." If you have spent ten difficult minutes lining up four tumblers, only to lose them all when the wrench skids, you may find yourself fitting and even hammering a taper nose wrench in on the next job.

Keyways with extremely limited access or low cross-section also benefit from a plug wrench that is slightly taper-cut to "bite" into the cylinder core.

The other category of wrench that crosses these two sets is the loose tip with rigid shank. It is usually produced by sloppy grinding of the tip and/or taper. Perhaps you will produce some by default. What will not fit your intended lock may still fit another smaller keyway, so don't deep six it in a fit of pique. As to the working quality of such a wrench, I can't even get started with it, but it may be worth a try for someone with a totally different style, kind of like an orthopedic wrench. Always give any tool system a trial before discarding it as unusable for your "fist," since once discredited in your mind you will probably never try it again. Experimentation produces failure, but it is also father to new tool design.

As you tool up on tight-fitting wrenches, you will soon find that the tight-fitting nose of one size of keyway is the sloppy fit of another keyway, with as little as .004″ of thickness difference. To deal with this problem, which is unique to tight-fit wrenches, a fair number of sizes of plug wrench in smoothly increasing increments and arranged in order will be necessary to work most types of lock with the same touch or fist that you prefer. The more gradual the taper, the larger number of sizes needed. A very steep taper tends to see-saw in the keyway, since it only bites at the very edge, and is to be strictly avoided. If you see-saw at a critical moment, you will zipper tumblers.

A = largest dimension of the fat tool
B = smallest dimension of the fat tool
C = largest dimension of the skinny tool
D = smallest dimension of the skinny tool

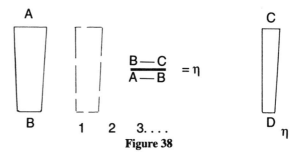

$$\frac{B-C}{A-B} = \eta$$

Figure 38

Note that a very shallow taper means a slightly tighter keyway fit, but means many more wrenches to make a full set.

For starters you can follow Figure 38 and produce a set of tools to dimensions that match most of the locks that will come under your hand. But even when entering a keyway system blind, (that is, starting from scratch with no patterns and dimensions), it is still easy to produce quickly a working set that can then be used as a baseline for future tool producing. You have the customary sets of code listings which will give keyway data, bitting increments and tumbler spacings, but not all locks are listed. Sometimes the books are just wrong, and some books are way too expensive to buy. Because of these reasons, starting from scratch is not all that bad.

Start with the fattest keyway you have in your plug collection, and produce a wrench that will wedge well in it. Measure the least and most dimensions of this tip, and also the least/most of a tool that fits the smallest keyway you could find. Now take the least of the fat tool (smallest portion of wedge) and the most (largest wedge) of the skinny tool and do the subtraction math. Take this figure and circle it, it is the theoretical full span of keyway widths you have seen to date. Now do subtraction between the two figures of each wrench (least/most) and notice this difference. This is the figure an average wrench wedge spans. Divide your circled figure by this average wrench span, and you will have a good idea of the number of steps or wrenches that will need to be created to fit most of the locks you would commonly encounter, assuming the taper angles on the wrenches remain fairly constant.

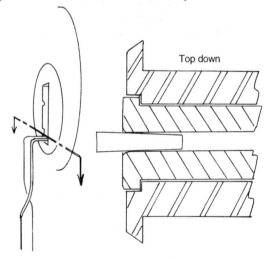

Figure 39
Showing taper fitting tight only at front.

Figure 39 shows you a top-down view of a tapered side wrench in a keyway and jammed tight. Since most keyways have some measurable wear, there will be a slight taper at the extreme outer mouth

and the taper usually seats well here. Consider, though, that any tapered tool will never contact anything more than the first .015″ of any parallel slot, which is what a keyway really is, and a truly parallel and tight fit is nearly impossible in anybody's daily work.

Given this tenuous hold, the smaller the angle of taper the better. Not that it will contact a much greater area of the keyway, because it won't. It will instead wedge much harder into the keyway and increase the feel feedback you look for in a tight-taper plug wrench. With approximately a two- to three-degree taper, one wrench will serve five to eight keyway sizes, and will even have to be removed forcibly at times. Remember that this raises burrs on the keyway that may accelerate key wear and tip someone to a picking attack.

Polished ground drill-rod blank stock is usually shipped soft, but sometimes it is supplied in a fairly hardened state and must be annealed or heated to cherry and slowly cooled before it can be bent at an angle. To test for this, try to cut a small bite with the triangle file somewhere in the middle of the rod. If it cannot be cut, it must be annealed. Once it is bent and cooled it is filed with two flats as usual, and then rehardened and tempered.

For a hard approach (not the best idea, just one idea) to the plug wrench problem, have you considered making some out of brass bar stock? In the .020″-and-up thicknesses there is no appreciable strength in it, but that is an advantage for us as it can be easily formed, and is naturally more springy. You can either cut your tight-fitting wrenches from brass rod stock with opposing flats just like a steel wrench, or you can grind a flat style wrench from the thin or thick variety of flat stock. If the stock thickness is less than .025″, the tongue of the wrench can be produced by folding over a long tab. It is even possible to make wrenches from brass angle stock (hobby store). The great advantage of the brass rod style wrench is its ability to not mar the keyway during rough insertion of the wedge-type wrench nose. Brass grinding, especially the alloy that is trade named "free-cutting brass," will load up the wheel a lot and requires frequent dressing.

To cut a few pieces of drill-rod stock easily in quick succession, you may go to the grinding wheel and do the same edge grind you do for shim stock. The method we use involves the oxyacetylene torch. If you play an intense, oxygen rich flame at the wire, it will quickly cherry up, and in another five seconds sparks will begin to fly from the surface. This indicates the steel is literally burning up as it begins to melt. In another second the steel drops from its own weight and, *Presto!*, one piece cut off with minimal effort. If the heating is slow enough to heat the wire past where bare hands can hold it, it is too slow. I arrange the torch in a clamp so both hands are free, and I use a wax pencil (china marker) to strike off lengths quickly on the rod surface. There will be a little cratering and burn around the melted area, but this is unimportant for a plug wrench tip, and can be ground off during final finish.

The steel pieces cut off should be arranged to NOT drop into the olive oil quench bath, since the advantage of this method is that it anneals the steel at the same time. Allow the pieces to collect on your fire brick or pumice pan. Once all the needed pieces are processed, heat them all to cherry red so as to complete the annealing.

To make the 85-degree bend in the wrench shank from these pieces you'll need a bending jig. Drill a hole $1/8''$ diameter and $3/8''$ deep into a piece of steel which is about 4-6'' on a side. The torch flame should be focused just parallel with this jig so the wire shank can be inserted into the hole, and quickly bent, then reversed, and double-bent. The wrench end points away from the direction of bending for the double bend. Notice that the torch heat is just an aid to easy bending and smooth radiusing. Heating has nothing to do at this point with hard or soft at all. If you are also offsetting each wrench tip size to make left- and right-hand wrenches, then the small offset bend should be put in each tip now, using the same bending jig. A skilled worker can make both bends using residual heat from one to facilitate the other. Allow cooling to continue in areas you don't desire to bend by re-reversing the wrench. The preferred sequence is insert, push away to 85, remove, reverse ends and insert, push away to 85. Re-reverse ends and insert, heat and 60-degree bend offset to left, again reverse ends, insert and 60-degree bend to right. Wear gloves.

Examine all the wrenches to see if both legs are in the same plane. If they are not, now is the time to straighten them. Apply a little heat to the middle of the wrench and give a slight twist in the required direction. Once straight, quench in the oil. The legs must lie in the same plane for the filing to be accurate. Now place all of the wrenches in line on the soldering block, and anneal all of their working ends up past the bend by heating to cherry red, then allowing to cool slowly to room temp. Customarily, one goes to lunch while they are cooling. The annealing is necessary because the next process is filing flats on the wrench.

If your wrenches are to be carried in a wallet, you may find it is useful to make a single-ended wrench with an eye at the end. This eye is bent into the rod using a pair of round-nose pliers on it while heated cherry red. The pliers will sink a lot of heat away from the rod, but the bend can still be accomplished in one or two stages with some dexterity. The diameter of the eye will depend on how far up or down on the round nose the wire is formed. A soapstone mark on the pliers helps to gauge this.

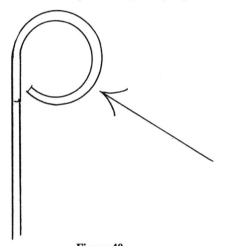

Figure 40
Hot-forming eye in wire end of wrench for chain/cord carry.

Once the eye is formed, it is heated cherry red again, and placed on its side on the bench pin anvil. It is then flattened with a mushroom or riveting hammer, alternating blows on either flat of the eye, while periodically reheating in the torch flame. The final step in eye forming is to heat and then hold the eye as in Figure 40 and close down the eye. It is wise to have a sample gauge rod of the wire you intend to string the wrench eye on, to verify it will still go on easily after this closing. If not, reform the eye. This blacksmithing technique can be made more handsome in appearance by filing the eye flat on both sides. Most tooling dents left by the hammer strikes are removed. This also allows the wrenches to register well on each other in a pack, or register on washers separating them in the pack. If you make a large pack, the washers may be stamped with numbers or points to indicate which size wrench is coming up. If you are thinking about trying it, this eye-flattening technique will also work on the tip of the plug wrench, but in practice little work is saved as opposed to straight filing, and the tip is pretty fairly deformed by such hammering. It is best to file only. I find that apprentices are unwilling to file anything major simply because they don't just dive in and start counting strokes. The sooner eighty strokes are started, the sooner it's done. A sure sign of an impatient file worker is the short stroke using only the middle of the file. If proper filing technique is used, even the hardest job is manageable.

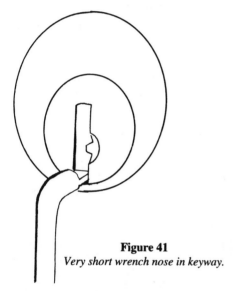

Figure 41
Very short wrench nose in keyway.

Notice in Figure 41 a wrench with a very short leg is shown inserted into a keyway. In most keyways milled into plugs, the bottom is left open to the inner wall of the cylinder. This is a natural result of the milling process. If a short wrench wedges only at the very front of the keyway, it can pivot on that bearing, and the end may either extend up into the keyway until it hits a ward, or it may pivot downward. If it pivots downward it can, if short, dig into the wall of the cylinder and cause considerable drag between plug and cylinder. It creates a mechanical connection between the two that inhibits free rotation. This drag will fatally short circuit the picking feel and the result is usually a non-opening. This drag problem is ruinous to good picking technique. The solution is to ensure that the leg of the plug wrench is long enough to only touch at a slight glancing angle to the cylinder wall. In addition, the end of the wrench should be

carefully radiused, almost angled, as shown in Figure 42, to prevent any cutting contact. As you do an opening, check occasionally to see if the plug wrench is hitting the cylinder wall. If it does, try making the bend in the wrench less by five degrees at a time. This makes the vector of force you apply to the wrench tend to push the wrench tip up into the keyway. It also forces the plug down in the cylinder (if the lock is mounted correctly with tumbler ends down), but really doesn't seem to help the tolerance any.

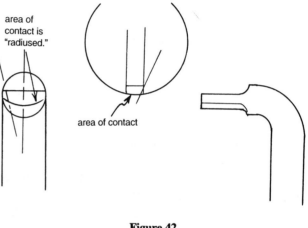

area of contact is "radiused."

area of contact

Figure 42
Cutting away wrench nose to prevent plug wall "drag."

Before starting to file flats on the wrench to complete it, some projected target should be written down and provisions made so it can be measured for as filing moves along. If you have a particular lock keyway in mind, use a set of modified feeler gauge leaves to measure the width of the slot. A regular automotive or machinist's set of feeler gauges in a jackknife-type pack can be used for this crucially important measurement. I say "crucially" because the jam fit of the wrench tip can be materially altered in feel either way by variations of as little as a .005".

To modify the pack for these measurements do this. Hold the entire pack closed and cut all of the leaves narrower in width until they are $3/32''$ wide. Do this on the wet grinder. Once this is done, make a couple of passes on the cut with the #4 mill file to even up the grind, and disassemble the pack. Now clean up every leaf individually with the India stone and oil to remove burrs. This pack can now be reassembled and inserted singly or in combination into a keyway to get a direct reading as to thickness of a plug wrench tip desired. The smaller width prevents keyway warding from blocking insertion of the feelers.

As noted in the lock pick-lifter height discussion, once a few sizes have been established to work, the rest of the system can be extrapolated and filled in, then tested in the field to see what is common and what is not.

Now that a target size has been decided, let's learn the technique of file-fitting a plug wrench. This procedure is done on the bench pin with the tension pin extended up.

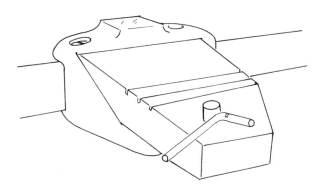

Figure 43
Using bench pin tension to hold wrench for filing.

Place a wrench blank on the bench pin, butted up against the tension pin as in Figure 43. The pin may be hammered down low as needed as long as it supports the wrench shank. Begin by choosing a narrow-edge, double-cut file and filing two notches in the wrench just past the bend. Look at Figure 44. These relief cuts should be only as deep as the projected final width. To gauge them easily, use the 4-way dial caliper. Their purpose is to allow the flat-cutting file to run parallel to the bench pin. If it were cutting against the wrench close to the bend, the cut would be angled and the tip would be much thinner, even though you try to control the file. By making relief cuts the file rides evenly on the steel, and the cuts also alert you when you are almost to the target width and should slow down the process. The first flat cut is made with your #4 file with the safe edge

riding on the bench pin. When the cut is completed, insert a trial-size or multiple sizes of thickness gauge in the space formed by the newly cut flat and the bench pin surface. To make the measurement, push down firmly on the uncut shank, floating the cut nose portion above the bench pin surface. When the exact thickness to match the amount of metal removed is reached, use this pack to block up under the wrench for the second flat cut. It will make the cut nearly parallel by eliminating rocking. Now make the second cut, stopping again as the relief groove is reached and obliterated. It will be impossible to make the wrench flats parallel with each other on a repeatable basis, but the taper must always go from fat outside the lock to thin inside. The small taper actually works to your advantage because it makes the fit-up much tighter.

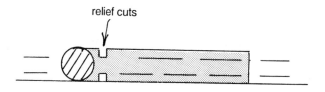

relief cuts

Figure 44
Location of initial cuts for finish-fitting-wedge-type tension wrench nose.

After filing as many wrenches as you require, they should be emery-papered or stoned well to remove all tooling marks. This is just as important with the wrench as it is with a lock pick because a rough wrench will sometimes stick when wedged tightly in a keyway, and removal sometimes breaks off a very brittle wrench in the plug. If this happens you get to use that key extractor you carry, if it works. After stoning, dip the wrench in olive oil, light the torch, then hold each wrench tip and bend in the flame, shank parallel to flame axis. By skipping the flame in a small arc on and off the tool, it will slowly and evenly heat to a dull red. The olive oil will act as an indicator, flaring to fire just before dull red heat is reached, or you may also use a small magnet to verify when tempering heat has been reached as the steel will lose its magnetic attraction at that precise point. When evenly heated, drop the wrench back in the oil bath. The bath should be checked periodically for temperature. If it is bathwater warm it will not quench properly and must be cooled before continuing. You can use two baths, both in metal containers, and keep one in the fridge at all times. As with picks after quenching, do not flex the wrench even gingerly, because most all of them will promptly snap off. Wait until after the draw tempering to see how strong they are. It seems that many of my students have roving fingers and idly or absently flex a freshly quenched tool; perhaps to see just how hard it really is. That slip can cost a half-hour of wasted tool time. I keep all such breaks in a glass jar on the bench just as a reminder to use kid gloves.

After the quench, the wrenches need to be tempered by heating to a light straw color. To accurately assess this, paper-polish an area the length of the pick. Set your torch for a very light, brushy neutral flame, or use just an alcohol lamp. Begin by heating the wrench NOT at the very tip, but at the mid-point of the mass that comprises the bend. It is okay for the very tip to be hard, but if the bend is brittle, it will fracture. The heating must initially be done very, very slowly, since the full spectrum of colors can suddenly bloom and fade in a hot spot, and that wrench must then be rehardened and retempered. I'd advise you to take at least a full two minutes in the beginning, slowly flicking the wrench in and out of the flame, trying to get thin and thick cross-sections to the same temperature at the same time.

The first color you will see will be a ghostly light straw. If heated further the colors will go to dark straw, peacock, then blue, and finally soft gray. I like to use my wrenches at that peacock color, and I have only lost one by stress fracture in twenty years. After some experience you can tell when the parade of colors is going to begin and you can slow down the heat even more. It does no harm to wait on a temper. Go fast and you must begin over again. Once the desired color/hardness combination has been reached, quench the wrench in water. That quench will not reharden it, it just retards further softening.

Once tempered, the tool should be cleaned of firescale with a fine emery or a cotton buff, and the wrench is done.

To produce the new-style, tight-nose spring shank wrench you must make a composite tool. A composite consists of two or more pieces joined with a wire rivet, usually nickel silver. Each piece is selected because it is close to the final size wanted, so no heavy cutting is required.

Learning to rivet is a skill you will find useful for adding handles and doing picks with pocket clips. If you can afford to learn ONE new skill this year, make it riveting. Joining two pieces of metal with a rivet allows for a lot of style variation and makes for more workable tools. In some cases a rivet is the only reasonable answer to a problem. Here is a good example. Suppose you wanted that composite wrench with a really tight wedging nose, and a springy shank. Here's how.

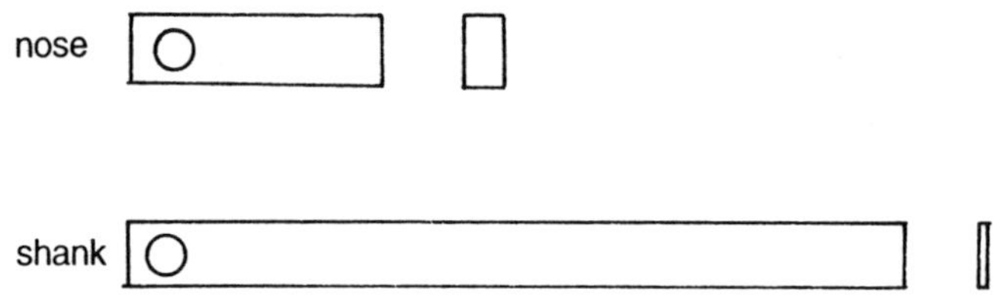

nose

shank

Figure 45
Composite (folding) tension wrench pieces comparative thickness.

The nose piece of a composite wrench is either precision ground flat stock or drill rod. Both are available from the usual industrial suppliers, and the flat stock comes in a variety of sizes and a few alloy types. I prefer 0-1 alloy, and the rough piece size is $3/32''$ thickness and saw/file as needed from the bar. Notice the hole drilled for the rivet in Figure 45. Flat-round stock comes soft, so annealing is usually not necessary. Drill the hole first and then file the nose to its desired size. A machinist's clamp will be a great holding aid for this small piece. If you are only doing three or four, you can make the holding easier by working the end of the bar into a nose shape, drilling the rivet hole, then hacksawing off the piece. The hacksaw cut can be cleaned up easily on the wet grinder or by bench filing. The nose should also be stoned for the nicest feel in the keyway.

The shank is cut from .030″ shim stock as per Figure 45.

The end will, of course, have to be annealed to allow drilling for the matching rivet hole. Once this piece is finished to size it must be rehardened all over and then drawn to a peacock or blue temper. The rivet is cut and inserted as per instructions in Chapter Ten.

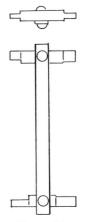

Figure 46
Four nose double-ended folding tension wrench.

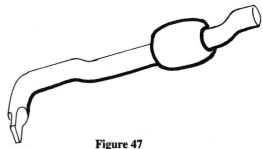

Figure 47
Wrench with captive weight secured by bends.

To use drill rod instead, follow these instructions. Select a piece of drill rod with a diameter equal to the top to bottom distance of the keyway slot area you are trying to fill. First cut the parallel opposing flats with the vise grip jig or other alternative. Now get out your torch and small-faced hammer, and a bench anvil. Heat the area one inch back from the flats to bright cherry and flatten it down with the hammer. Remove from the quench bath and use a mill file to dress off any hammer mars and dents, and cut one whole face flat. Into the middle of this face, drill a rivet hole of appropriate diameter. Now resmooth that face and file a radius on the rivet end of the small rod nose piece you have just created. Finally, reheat to cherry and quench. Temper to peacock. The flexible shank is cut from shim stock, the end of which is annealed and drilled prior to any layout. Drill to match the rivet hole in the nose, of course. After layout and grinding, the shank is heated to cherry, quenched and tempered to blue. Finally the rivet is fabricated to length, oiled, assembled, riveted, de-greased and dressed down.

This tension wrench offers the best of both worlds, and the shank response is very even. As a bonus this wrench may be folded up flat and carried easily in the watch pocket. For the dedicated tinkerer this same wrench may be made in a double-nosed version shown in Figure 46. Also pictured is a double-ended, double-nosed type. While this may look like a gimmicky little pocket piece, it is actually very handy. The protruding nose gives the locksmith something to grab hold of in order to release a tightly wedged nose.

Once assembled, this wrench must be adjusted to your own unique fist. This is done slowly at first. Attempt a few openings on locks at the shop or ones you are already familiar with at your established accounts. I have a friend who works mostly downtown in the garment district, and he knows the pin order, feel and quirks of a lock on the security gate of the money vault of an established account. Whenever he is called there for a lost key box service, he picks the lock on the grill to gain access. He could easily ask for the key, but he gains practice and uses it to try out new tools. Most importantly, it enhances his reputation at the bank immensely by the off-handed way he says, "Don't bother hunting up the key. I'll just open this lock right up!"

Anyway, to develop your fist measurement, start by opening with the plug wrench as is. If it feels too stiff, take a light grinding cut off the outside edge of the shank and restone it down to remove the burrs. Continue this process until you feel you may have gone too far. At that point you can either unrivet the shank and replace with a new shank pre-cut to the last width you liked, or keep the wrench shank as is and recut the nose for a different keyway.

Once you have established some sense of where your fist is and what tool produces that feel, you can make as wide a variety of plug wrenches with different nose sizes as you need, and pre-cut them to your personal taste.

The subject of weighted tension wrench handles is last to be looked at. The weight is most frequently a lead fishing sinker with the wire eye removed and the core hole redrilled to a little over the drill-rod diameter. The weight may be fixed at one spot on the wrench handle or moveable within a region. There are lock pick technicians who swear by a weighted wrench, and others who leave them strictly alone. It is just another example of tools having to give way to technique. If it helps you, good; if not, don't force liking it.

Those who use a weighted wrench say it offers more sensitive feel on a rigid shank wrench, a sensitivity they don't get with a slimmer, more springy wrench shank. This is again an individual thing. But weight is definitely good in one respect for applying perfectly consistent tension on a lock. Two situations that cause no end of trouble are the non-automotive sidebar locks and brand spanking new high-tolerance, pin-tumbler locks. The sidebar wants the least tension possible, and the new lock needs it unvarying. To attack a sidebar, try a weight that only just causes a tumbler to hang at the shear, and increase it just a touch (this is a sliding type). The advantage here is that you can do it in the field. Even better, if the wrench is calibrated you can note the level and use it again on that same or similar locks.

To weight a drill rod wrench, bend and flat grind onto one end only, and leave the shank straight. After marking the rod, drilling the sinker and threading it on, the little torch can be used to run quick bends in the rod effectively trapping the sinker on. A bend pair can be spaced in different ways and on different parts of the shank to suit the maker. See Figure 47 for details.

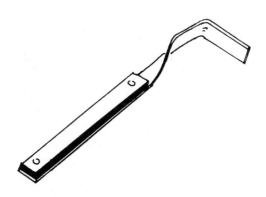

Figure 48
Added handle material to weight flat-style wrench.

For a friction fit with no bends, just swedge the ends of the weight down with a hammer and pin-punch. The sliding weight may be matched to a much-longer-than-usual wrench, if you can verify the wrench won't butt into any adjoining door jamb. But, if this is found to be the case, some judicious bending

may save the day. Put the shank end at, say, 1:30 o'clock instead of 3:00 o'clock. For long slides, a series of small nicks should be marked off with layout dye and dividers set by rule, and successively filed in the BOTTOM of the shank with a three-corner file. This allows reference to be made.

If you want to do some research into which weight might be better for a certain lock (probably those sidebars again), the notches can be filed on the TOP of the shank and different-weight sinkers with wire loops attached can be rested in those notches for graduation of turning force. If you get a weight combo you really like, take the torch and bend an eye at that "sweet" spot, effectively trapping the weight there. This allows you to use the wrench for both left and right openings.

Even if you do not like weighted wrenches, you should consider carrying a single weight with a large wire loop still attached. If you have to move around, loosen a cramped-up shoulder, or even leave the lock for a few minutes altogether, the weight slung on the wrench will keep tension on the core and keep your two pins picked without having to start all over.

As to weighting a flat-style, loose nose tension wrench, the only practical approach seems to be riveting on a $^1/_{16}''-^1/_8''$ piece of flat stock as in Figure 48. Any other approach may likely unbalance the wrench's center of gravity and make it hard to maintain a good camming fit in the keyway.

One bonus to the use of a weighted tension wrench is that you can leave it hanging in the door instead of leaving yourself hanging in case things get hot. You know the problem — you get tired, the hand slips, you hear the night watchman, you have to go... and you have four out of five pins gimmicked; what frustration to have to "zipper" that lock and start over!

Previous books and such talk about weights and thumbtacks with rubber bands, but there is a better way. Another related problem is the extremely narrow keyway that only a severely cut-down wrench will work in. To counter this you can try tweezers or straddle wrenches, but many slip out at times, usually the worst of times. There is a better way.

Get thee to the local bearing shop. Ball/roll-er/needle bearing suppliers are in the yellows. Electric-motor repair shops junk noisy but perfectly good bearings. The local auto graveyard also is good if you are a mechanic of sorts. The target is a small, thin assembly, unshielded, about 2" outside diameter and as large as possible inside (shaft) diameter. Figure 49 shows you the idea. The two posts or teeth are small Allen wrenches set into drilled holes in the inner race. It is usually necessary to soften (anneal) this very hard alloy steel. The retaining screws are set into holes drilled perpendicular to the Allen wrench holes. The second set of holes is tapped for a 4/40 screw. This allows the teeth to be set in many different attitudes, and other teeth to be inserted as well for varying lock styles and keyways. The third hole (outer race) accommodates the tension spring. The fourth and fifth holes are just through holes to fit the nails and such that will affix the tension ring to the door in question.

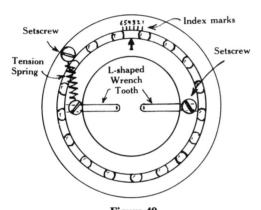

Figure 49
Ball-bearing tension wrench.

Ever wonder what good those burglar etching tools were? Well, get one (actually use your carbide-layout scriber) and engrave a scale of 1-7 or whatever on the outer race and a register mark (called a witness) on the inner race. This is done after the tool is completed.

I carry several types of tooth and tooth tips that have been useful over the years, and a blank set left soft to file on the job for new locks. Each set of tips must be bent to mostly the same contour, so use the Allen wrench as supplied, or modify it by torch-bending and match the teeth side-by-side for corrections. In fact, try to bend both tips as one unit using pliers or toolmaker's clamp.

By contrast, the different tips on the teeth are almost never the same in contour. Most keyways are different in bottom and top contours, and the tips must be a jam fit. Remember to allow maximum clearance for the pick, which is the whole idea.

Ideally, you should position the teeth so the center of rotation of the plug is also the center of rotation of the wrench. If one tooth is very long and one is very short AND the tips fit real tight, there will be trouble as the plug turns (isn't that a soap?).

The engraved scale is used, of course, to track what tensions are good for what types of locks and what types of picks. Track the numbers by lock type and try to tell if the lock was lubricated lately. This will throw off the numbers a lot. Coil springs must be occasionally changed to match the type of lock as well. Hobby shops carry some, and coils may be clipped off to make the spring tighter. If you have two springs and don't know which is looser, hook them together and pull. The looser one springs out first and farther. Stretching the spring will make it respond differently over a wider pull area.

To make the scale show up in low light, try pick-nail polish rubbed in and wiped when dry. A gun sight ramp can be so treated to help you pick it up faster in low-light conditions, too. This idea even extends to any of your blued picks. Touch coding for night use was covered in Chapter Ten; here we are talking about a white dot or series of stripes to find the tool if you drop it in the black grass.

Aha, you are saying, how does this whole thing attach to the door? Well, a couple of grinder-sharpened light nails with large heads will go through the two holes in the outer race nicely if the door is made of wood. For a steel door, make a corral or fence around the bearing with a few magnets, or epoxy a magnet right to the ring. For some other doors neither dodge works well. Some decorator doors have irregular trim or plates. To get the ring to stick here a sub mount is necessary. Drill a hole in a piece of ¼"-thick paneling exactly the size of the outer race, and insert same into said wood hole. Use epoxy to make the bond. The wood will now hold by friction if you keep it in place, or it may be nailed or even taped.

The larger well-to-do homes sport these difficult doors, and this reminds me of a strategy you should know.

Two things happen as a luxury home or subdivision is built. Number one, the spec sheet on hardware is specific on brand only. This is often an industry standard like Schlage or Yale. The actual type and model of lock is left to the builder and his spec sheet will be the cheapest that complies. I know one entire subdivision where the contractor put in

Schlage wafer-tumblers. The Schlage spec was met, but the security was delightfully low, low, low. Even die-cast pin-tumblers would have been better.

The second thing is related to the first. In any subdivision you can bet that all of the locksets initially will be the same type and model. Builders employ semi-skilled tradesmen to install locking hardware, and rarely keep track of key codes. This means one set of lock tools will be sized for the entire area. The only exception is the do-it-yourself nut who puts on high-security deadlocks, pry-resistant, electronics and so on. This is rare. The busy rising professional does not have time to do lock work, and this means the busy mechanic can more efficiently do his job. The younger in age the subdivision, the less likely alterations have taken place, or that locksets have corroded or jammed. A call to the builder will disclose the hardware jobber who supplied the locksets, and you may then get one "to match my front door, please."

This also holds true for garage and window locks. This is important to you because you remembered to attack the weakest link in the security chain, right? Finally, scope out subdivisions with large numbers of music/intercom systems installed during construction. Such houses may also have security systems made by the intercom supplier. Such packages are often done hand-in-hand, and even share some components. Builders who offer these are still using the same tradesmen to install, and they will follow a set, learned pattern. The sensors, panel locations, and wiring conventions will be very similar. Why should the guy change a good thing that works for him? If you can chart just one or two of these installations, you will have a better working knowledge for other locations. The locking systems will also be standard and the jobber easily located. If it turns out not to be a jack-of-all-trades-type jobber but someone who ONLY deals security, obviously you should proceed with more caution. You are relying, however, on the builder being unwilling to go to many different suppliers, and the least common denominator is what he usually chooses.

Chapter Twelve
Jeweler's Grinding Tools

The designs of lock-opening tools may occasionally call for a very narrow slot to be cut into the middle of the steel blank, like the tool in Figure 50. This figure shows a double-pronged tool to be used as a tension wrench on a wafer-tumbler lock with double-key bitting. This width of slot could be cut from the side using a corner of the grinding wheel and cleaning up with a file, but that's very time consuming. For an even *more* extreme tool problem, examine this next figure also. Figure 51 shows a double-bitted profile pick with an even narrower slot cut down the middle. The function of the slot is to impart a small amount of "give" or flex to both sides of the tool. Many locksmiths rely on this design because it works so well on the types of double-bitted, disc-tumbler lock in which each side of the bitting is coded independently of the other side. Such a lock cannot be raked by holding two tools loosely in one hand and using them together. To duplicate this tool is thus desirable, but what about that tiny slit? Very thin slit-cutting on the edge of the grinding wheel is not practical, so a different approach is required. It is also difficult to find a file cut to this narrow width, and remember that hardened steel can be only ground or filed, not cut with any jeweler's or similar saw. The answer is the jeweler's sprue or cutoff wheel.

The average locksmith will be unfamiliar with them, but people in the jeweler's trade routinely use these abrasive wheels composed of rubber with embedded abrasive grains, usually closely graded silicon carbide. "Brightboy" is a trade name. In addition to these soft wheels, there are a variety of other semi- to hard wheels like the "Mizzy" brands and others. All of these are in the ½″ to 1½″ diameter range, and they are designed to be mounted on a set of minuscule arbors that are chucked into flexible shaft handpiece machines. This tool is mounted in the handpiece or drill and is designed to sever the sprue or "flash" attached to a finished item of cast metal jewelry after its removal from the plaster mold. The small stub left on the piece by the wheel is artfully removed by filing. Jeweler's cutoff wheels are capable of cutting high-carbon steel, yet the cut-off wheels are $^1/_{32}″$ thick at the face. They are also used to execute jewelry designs in three dimensions by carving. The catch in using these wonderful abrasives is that they work best at 5,000 + r.p.m.'s, so a flexible shaft handpiece or handheld grinder is necessary for their efficient use. These shaft grinders are not cheap. You are welcome to try using the abrasives in a regular drill, but the results will be very disappointing. There are two respected names for those flexible shaft machines: "Vigor" and "Foredom." There are also air-driven die grinders but I found them either unsuitably heavy and uncontrollable for this delicate work, or light but ver-r-ry expensive.

The large price tag to purchase one of these highly specialized tools may not immediately be appealing to someone looking to execute only a dozen tools per month, but our Foredom has been in use over six years and it is highly useful in many other delicate locksmithing operations. It has the necessary flexibility and high r.p.m.'s to do a lot of jobs that are customarily done with other tools. We have used it for polishing key burrs, light rust removal, surface finishing, slot-machining in tight spots, and even precision hole-drilling in the #60-80 range. It is unexcelled for polishing brass padlock cases to conceal a set of newly plugged pin wells. I am confident that many locksmiths will find many more uses for such a tool in their shops also, so consider adding one to the bench.

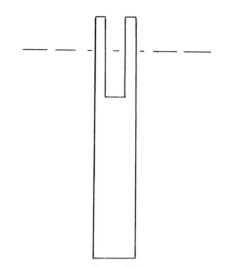

Figure 50
Bend site of slotted steel to make 2-pronged wrench.

Figure 51
Slot to make pick bitting sides "flex" independently.

Another handpiece type tool is used for grinding. It is called the Cratex-type wheel. It is like a miniature grinding wheel, and its use is the technique of choice for rough grinding to very complex layout lines. Lock picks like the rocker and the snake pick executed in shim steel benefit from the use of a Cratex-type wheel. For this work the handpiece can be clamped to the bench top or held in a device designed for just such a purpose.

For all-around pick finishing, slotting and dimensioning there is no better tool than a Foredom and a set of Cratex or cutoff wheels. These abrasives allow almost infinite control over the small amount of material to be removed, so that blueprint standards of thousandths of an inch can be repeatably machined to. The grinding wheel will customarily rough out to within ten or twenty thousandths, and the Cratex will finish the job.

These soft rubber abrasives (Cratex) come in a wide variety of shapes, grits, and face widths. I prefer

to stock and use a $^1/_8''$ face straight wheel of 2″ diameter in fine grit, and a tapered edge, fine grit $^5/_8''$ wheel for finishing into the tight corners of Diamond picks. You will need a ¼″ and $^1/_{16}''$ mandrel or arbor to mount both of these wheels. They have an occasionally unfortunate tendency to catch on the hard wire edge left by the rough grinding wheel, and strip or spiral their little guts out. Given the very low price of the wheels, it isn't worth worrying about. There is not enough torque to catch and hurl a pick when this happens, but I usually have my picks clamped in a bench vise by their handles anyway. I do this so that I may quickly switch from finishing to mikeing and back again, almost a left-to-right-back-to-left-handed operation. You can also clamp the grinder handpiece in a vise or bench clamp and secure your micrometer in a padded jaw bench mount, switching the pick between the two. This works especially well if your mike has a spindle lock so it can be converted into a temporary go-no-go gauge. Most dial calipers also have a grub-screw slide lock, and may be better for this operation.

I have done some experimentation with executing the rough grinding outlines by cutting the steel from the side (the face) with a small cut-off wheel or a "Mizzy" wheel. This is to save time as compared to overgrinding away the edge. The results are so-so. It is certainly easier to clamp a pick into a grinding jig and edge grind as usual down to the finished form, since this can be done without holding the steel. It is also true that any pet projects or extra-special outlines you may wish to experiment with seem to be easier cut from the side. Try it once or twice and see what you think. It is possible to hold the pick down onto a large steel bench block using a couple of rare earth magnets while grinding from the side. It is also possible to use mist coolant on this arrangement as well. Remember that excessive heat will weaken or destroy the magnetism, so don't try this unless you cool also. Coolant seeping into the precision bearings of your Foredom handpiece will destroy it. To dry it out after such grinding, run it at full speed for ten minutes to get it hot and the water usually evaporates. All things considered, I prefer to rough-grind outlines on the bench wheel.

Note also that while fine-finishing to the layout line can be executed with a plain ol' finishing file, the motorized abrasive has two advantages: less chatter and fatigue on large jobs, and the ability to follow difficult and convoluted layouts, like snake or wiggly picks.

Now let's return to the first tool: the double-nosed plug wrench. The initial step in making this tool is making the 90-degree bend at one end. The steel may be clamped in a bench vise, toolmaker's clamp, or spring clamp to insulate the hand. A narrow band of steel is heated cherry red one inch from the end, and the bend quickly executed by grabbing the end with pliers and simultaneously bending and pulling, as if you wanted to stretch the steel on the long piece of steel. This pulling helps to make the bend's radius smaller by forming it more tightly along the clamp edge. If you can very quickly heat a very narrow band of steel to cherry, then the bend can be done by bopping the short end down on a workbench top, but this is hard to do. As the heat conducts away from the bend site it also softens the steel, and the result is a bend with a wider radius. The bend can be adjusted for angle by slightly reheating and nudging either way with the pliers' nose or jaws, and then the bend is heated cherry once more and plunged into an oil bath to leave it in the hardened state. It would be necessary to cherry-heat the entire tool to get it all hard uniformly again, but the only critical area of strength will be the tip and the bend, so it is easy to harden and temper these, and leave an area or band of soft steel down into the handle. The outside radius of the bend is immediately polished with emery cloth or felt buff to remove the scale, and the bend then gradually and fleetingly reheated until that shiny spot turns straw or peacock blue in color. When that color emerges it has been tempered. Now comes the part where a Cratex or flexible grinding wheel is vital: cutting a slot down the middle. The slot could be cut prior to bending, but the tines will align better this way, and the bend produces some rigidity to the piece which will make it easier to cut. The slot could also be cut when the steel is still annealed, but the grinding is not much different on hardened steel, and the hardening process applied to both prongs simultaneously would risk warping them out of their alignment. The slot you will cut allows working clearance for the pick manipulating the wafer or disc tumblers, and the degree to which you cut internally will define the approximate width of the tines to be inserted into the keyway. The final tine filing to fit occurs on the outside edges. A file would take a long time to cut such a wide and long slot, but the rubberized abrasive wheel makes short work of it.

Chapter Thirteen
Leather Cases

The choice of what type of case to carry your lock picks in should be based on one question: Will the picks be carried in a pocket or carried anywhere else? In a pocket means anywhere on or very near your person or clothing, and anywhere else means inside tool boxes, drawers, car glove compartments, etc. The downfall of a body- or person-carry is pick corrosion, and I will explain this.

The lock picks and related tools you can create after mastering the skills outlined in this manual will come only at a considerable investment in bench time and craftsmanship. They really should be well-protected, from the bending and possible breakage that may occur when you carry those tools on a daily basis. If well-protected, your personal lock picks will last your working lifetime. High-carbon steel should also be insulated from the high humidity that carrying them on your person will expose them to, or they will rust and pit. Just as an off-duty officer will carry his gun in a leather holster, the locksmith should consider nothing less than a top-quality, leather pick wallet as the home for personal precision tools.

Before covering personal cases, then, let's discuss the tool box and so on case. How would you like the ultimate high-tech pick cases; zippered all around for no tool fallout, padded sides, classy vinyl? Sounds good? Just take a drive down to the local Bible/Sunday School gift store and you will find Bible cases that easily will convert to pick-carrying cases. Take a pick or two (longer lengths) to test and you may find that certain brands will exactly fit two "racks" of picks placed side by side. While you are there pick up a generous assortment of tracts and pamphlets to bolster your "cover." Maybe even add a lapel button or pin; a neck chain is too obvious.

If you want to add a third leaf to the Bible case, or just need to reconfigure it, you must add to it with compatible material. The vinyl/foam dinner placemats with those cute pictures of duckies and horsies on them that are available everywhere will provide excellent material. The plastic is semi-rigid and easily cut, yet has a tough vinyl outer skin. When adding a leaf, sew it on with heavy carpet thread. Try to keep the duckies and horsies pictures imprinted on the placemat on the inside of the pick case. It pays to maintain a professional image, after all. Individual pick pockets may be outlined by sewing, or SOME types of glues will also work. Test to make sure the glue you choose will stand up to moderately heavy use without unsticking. If you have trouble with this, the vinyl can be cut: two slits both just $1/8''$ longer than the pick handle width, and spaced anywhere from $1/2''$ to $3''$ apart will make nifty loops for the picks to be bayonetted into. If your handle is coded you can make one a smaller slit for the pick tip and insert away from the open face of the case, avoiding the dreaded protruding pick-tip puncturing your anatomy. The tip then will not show, so coded handles alone will tell which is which.

The classic zippered case that you get with standard pick sets will be familiar to any working locksmith. They come in four flavors, up to one with two fold-out "wing" flaps. While this zipper design is good for keeping picks from straying, it can make it uncomfortable to carry, and a case that is bulky often gets left behind. A case of tools has not yet been invented that will get up, walk out the door and down to where you are waiting to use it. Nothing is more frustrating than to have built up solid lock picking skills and hand-crafted beautiful tools, and have them home in a drawer when you REALLY NEED to pop a lock.

After scouring numerous retail offerings of wallets, card cases, and small clutch purses for days, I came to the conclusion that the best way to get a case of the proper dimensions is either to make one for yourself, or find a leather craftsman who will sew one up. If you go the latter route it will materially reduce your craftsman's bill if you can provide a set of cutting templates made of frosted mylar material. Before I outline the procedure of template making, I will say that a standard credit card long wallet can be customized by adding a few pockets and slits here and there to make a passable substitute. You can choose this easy way out or get one sewn to specification, but at least read this chapter.

The outside dimensions of the case are easily worked out. Measure out a convenient pocket size for width; about 3½″ to 4″ is good. For length, remember that a foldover when open will be double the average pick or tension wrench length, both of which are 4–6″, plus ¼″. Since I prefer the longest tool I can comfortably carry, my case is sewn accordingly. Let me emphasize comfort. It is easy to make a case to carry lots and lots of tools and wrenches for locks you probably will only encounter once or twice in a year. To be sure of your dimensions, you can lay your picks out in any convenient order on the actual leather. If you are unsure of the process, the initial pick layout can be on heavy paper, cardboard or soft vinyl. A dining-table placemat is an excellent quickie source for foam sandwich vinyl. Experiment with pick layout until you come up with one that is workable. Remember that the smaller wire-tension wrenches can ride two in a recess cut. Also remember to leave sufficient margin all around the edges where stitches will be placed when the leather case is assembled. The number of flaps to add, pockets and so on is variable, and Figure 52 will give you an idea of the possibilities.

Once the layout is finalized either outline the tools with a marker pen on the leather or other pattern, or spray a single pass of layout dye over the pick array, which will accurately mark their layout. A notation in marker ink will remind you of what tool went where. I find it's also a good idea to make a high-quality photocopy of the finished pattern before cutting it out.

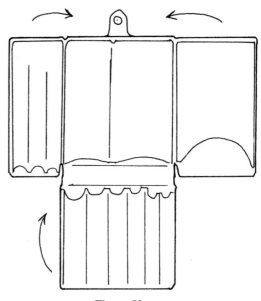

Figure 52
Case with foldable leafs.

If you have a paper pattern, cut with scissors and assemble with tape, then insert the tools and try to assess how well this layout works for you. If it's good, go on to the next step. If not, retry a new design.

Once the design is proved, cut it out and use it as a pattern to draw lines on the leather. You can move the pattern around to avoid rough spots, holes, rangemarks, and whatever. Now it's time to pick a leather to use for your case.

A leather craftsman's supply store should carry the following hides. Garment pigskin is easy to cut and sew, comes pre-dyed in a multitude of shades, and is inexpensive. It does have very little stiffness, and cases made from it will "flop" open just from the weight of four or five picks, but that is a matter of taste. The stiffness of pigskin can be increased by a combination process of dying with alcohol-based dye and then coating with a nitrocellulose lacquer. If you prefer to carry lots of different picks around, the thinner leather will keep total bulk down.

Morocco cowskin is much stiffer and so more difficult to sew and trace-cut. It comes only in a few colors, usually dark, and does not crease easily either, but it can be grooved to accept stitches. The trade-off is that this leather makes a case that holds its shape even without a pick inside. If you carry just a few picks, this is a good choice. Just try to thread a pick into a floppy pigskin case once and you will appreciate stiffness as a virtue.

Garment cowskin, sometimes called biker leather, combines qualities of the two other leathers. It is between the two in softness, creases well, sews easily with a glover's needle, and comes in a few colors. For my taste, it's the perfect choice for a cool CIA-type black bag.

If you carry picks with fairly thick handles, you may want a thick spacer. The spacer is cut from 8 oz. or thicker carving leather. It will stiffen ANY case, and its thickness gives an ample pocket for a big handled pick. A good combination is black garment outer case with a carving leather spacer.

Once you have decided on and purchased leather hides, the cutting process comes next. They sell a lot of specialty knives for the leather trade, some that will do intricate curves and bevels, but these are unneeded for most pick wallet designs. A razor blade is all you'll need for straight cutting leather on a board. If you want to lay out the pattern using fine-point pen on light leather or white art pencil on dark, a bandage or EMT emergency shear can be used to cut the leather in hand. Invest in a leather shear only if you have bucks to burn. After cutting out the pieces of the case, cut the spacer out as well.

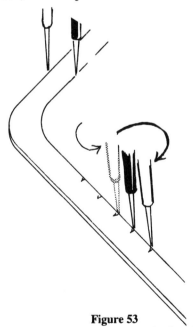

Figure 53
Compass points set for sewing seam set-back and stitch spacing.

Using the marker lines, cut away from the leather spacer where the tools will be housed. A couple of new, sharp Exacto knifes will do well here, as the

leather is very tough. Once the pockets or slots (if any) for the accommodation of the tool handles have all been cut, the top and bottom sides of the case are applied with glue or just held in place with paper clips used as clamps, until all of the holes for the stitching can be punched or awled into the top leather piece. A compass set to the correct seam inset, and the desired hole spacing as well, is an invaluable tool here. As shown in Figure 53, the sharp point of the compass will scribe a parallel line, and the same compass, set to whatever stitch spacing, can be also "spider-walked" along that line to mark hole locations.

A stitching spacer wheel in seven stitches per inch is nice to have. After the leather is cut, instead of using the dividers you can run this wheel along the lines to be stitched, and it will produce a series of perfectly spaced prick marks to guide your sewing. This can be done freehand for both straight lines and curves if your pattern requires it. An eight- or nine-stitch per inch wheel gives an even more finished appearance, but is hard to locate. The ones produced for fabric sewing don't leave a clear enough impression. The drawback to using the wheel is that it produces many more stitches that have to be done, where the divider is set usually to fewer stitches per inch, like four or five. If you get the really fine wheel you can just stitch every other hole if you wish.

Traditionally, the holes are either tube-punched or pierced with a mallet-driven awl, but with thinner leather and the proper stitching-awl as well, the leather may be directly sewn. Direct sewing is a tremendous time saver.

Needles to sew leather are either smooth or triangular. The smooth ones are numerous in name. Tapestry, crewel, and sharps are just a few of the labels, and all of these require a lot of force to pierce even the thinnest leather. The triangular needles are called glover's needles, and are designed to sew leathers for gloves. The triangle shape creates edges that cut like an awl, so the needle penetrates easily. With a thimble and a glover's needle leather, up to 2-2.5 oz. weights may be easily sewn. They are well worth running down to purchase.

Don't confuse sewing needles with thonging or lacing needles, both of which are much larger and useless for this finer caliber leather work.

Leather stitchers use a very heavy linen-based, twisted thread. For this neater case work, a carpet thread singled or doubled is better. Buy it at a sewing outlet, and if in doubt take your needle along to verify it will fit the thread.

A cake of beeswax can be had at either a leather or sewing supplier, and is used to lubricate, stiffen, and strengthen the thread before sewing. If you purchased a jeweler's saw and frame you will need the beeswax to lubricate the saw, so buy two cakes. By the way, Uncle Sam (you) pays a subsidy to beeswax growers every year, so do your patriotic duty: buy more beeswax and sweep the Axis from the waves.

A thimble is essential, even with a smooth-pushing glover's needle. The amount of force required to sew is still formidable, and sore fingers are no fun when picking locks or drinking shots. Make sure the thimble fits your index finger loosely, but will stay on when inverted. Another option is the sewing palm, a leather or plastic appliance with a metal insert which is fitted to the heel of your right hand, with a strap attached around your wrist. The metal insert is used to push the needle's butt through the leather once it is inserted. If you use a #3 glover's, it will be long enough to sew comfortably with a palm; the smaller ones are too short to do this well. Leather finger stalls (tubes) may also be useful, IF the stall leather is heavy enough. Buy a very stiff cowhide leather stall, not a limp one.

If you prefer, small needle-nosed pliers can also be used to sew with. This will both grip and push the needle through the leather and pull the needle and thread out the other side. You will either love it, or be unable to feel comfortable with it. Most of those who sew leather by hand for profit say they prefer the pliers.

A sewing pony is a clamp that holds the leather case so you don't have to. If you want to make one quickly, see Figure 54. The two boards are 1x4' pine, the spacer is a block of 2x4' and the bolt is anything with washers on the ends. The wedge that goes in the bottom pony mouth must be worked out until it fits correctly, but it is not difficult. The pony will make work easier if you do three or more cases.

The interior of the case where the pockets are cut should also be sewed, at least with a couple of tack stitches to prevent the case from becoming a large pocket with a piece of Swiss-cheesed leather that does not prevent the tools from mixing all together. To keep the pockets separated, sew their boundaries as well.

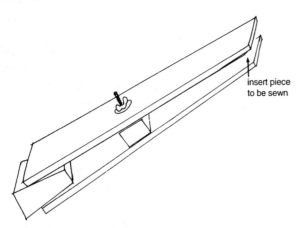

insert piece
to be sewn

Figure 54
Leather workers' sewing "pony" to hold work while stitching.

Chapter Fourteen
Pick Hilt Soldering

Pick handles are often altered by their owners from the as-supplied condition to something a little more comfortable or for heavier heft, or both. Enlarged or heavier handles are placed on the pick to give sufficient weight to counterbalance the pick comfortably for lifting. The counterbalancing is against the resistance of the tumblers being lifted. This weight must be considerable to balance against some tumblers.

The force of the tumbler springs is just a minor one compared to the resistance to tumbler lifting due to core and shell friction that the misalignment caused by the tension wrench creates.

Providing sufficient area for finger grips that can transmit feel and control in the directions most helpful to lock picking is another handle priority. While slab side or bent self-handles offer lots of possibilities, the best control is created by appliances affixed to the pick. These add-ons, such as finger rings, double handles, clips, or whatever, work so well because they extend well into the third dimension. Since they exert considerable leverage and have odd contours, they must be tightly secured to the lock pick handle, and the two best methods are silver-soldering and riveting. Riveting technique is covered in the chapter on handles, and here eddie discusses silver solder.

For a quick fix aimed more at better feel and not so much for weight, your first try will be to silver-solder a small piece of brass or nickel silver strip-stock to one or both sides of the pick handle. The brass may be crosswise similar to where a knife has its hilt or guard, or extend at any angle to the steel handle. Either type of brass add-on will be invaluable to you as a hand grip to control the movement of the pick in the lock, after having suffered with the plain old ¼"- to ½"-wide handle. The new process of silver solder is more accurately called silver brazing but nobody says brazing. Of the three hot join methods there is soft solder, hard solder or braze, and welding. The most notable thing about silver solder to remember is its very high melting/working temp. The melting temperature of the silver solder will vary according to which grade is chosen, and the chart below shows the five commonly available grades and their matching temps. There is a loose relationship between hardness of the solder and melting temperature, but the harder/hotter the working temperature, the more difficult it is to use for a beginner. The first few joints you make should be with so-called EZ or repair solder. If you can only go shopping for this at a hardware store, remember that silver solder is not to be confused with soft solder like the plumbers use on copper pipes. Soft solder has a lead base, and it will in no way adhere well to the shim steel. A jeweler's supply is the better place to get commercial silver solder. By the way, silver solder gets its name from its customary use by jewelers, to solder coin or sterling silver alloys. It actually will wet or merge with the molecular surface of the two pieces being joined, hence the superior joint strength it offers. It is one step below actual welding or fusion of the base metal.

Solder flow	degrees F
IT	1490
hard	1450
medium	1360
easy	1325
easy flow	1270
ready flow	1200

Silver solder made for the jeweler's trade comes in wire, piece, powder, and the kind we use: sheet form. Small pieces of this sheet are cut by making a series of parallel or fringing cuts into the sheet with snips, and then cutting crosswise to produce rectangles or squares. It is very important to label the type/temperature of solder when doing this. If two different temperatures of solder are used in the wrong sequence on one project, a previous colder solder joint may suddenly collapse when you are working on another area of the pick using a hotter solder. Put pre-cut pieces of solder in a pill bottle and label the bottle as to grade, and also label the uncut full sheet of solder with a felt tip pen.

Whichever solder temp. you choose and use, its melting point will be well above the soft annealing temperature range for the pick steel, so the steel pick must be protected by a heat sink, or large steel area between the joint and the critical handle-to-pick shank transition area, or both. The hilt handle will do the most good if placed closer to the front of the pick, so a heat sink is a necessary precaution. You can do the solder joint after the pick has been rough- or even-finish ground, but it is harder to hold and control the steel during rough grinding with a protruding hilt. On the other hand, there is more steel to absorb the heat and prevent problems if you solder before any grinding is done on the pick. That's assuming the handle does not project into the grinding wheel path, or hit any other obstructions.

Carbide-scribe the projected pick outline onto the steel, and then layout or measure where you want the guard to be and scribe its location as well. Do not use layout dye, as it will mask the joint. The mating surfaces of steel and brass or nickel and silver should be cleaned of oxide and grease by a light emery cloth buffing, followed by a swipe with a naphtha soaked rag. Unless the joint is perfectly clean, the solder will not flow well, and the joint may be flawed. After cleaning, apply flux to both surfaces and also to the small pieces of solder used in the joint. There are two types, paste and liquid flux mixtures, available. I prefer the solid borax and alcohol pastes because they retain their fluxing capacity a little longer than liquids. The common problem beginners have is in heating the joint overlong and losing the window of fluxing action. The resulting joint will be weak or non-binding. The paste form is more forgiving of this common problem. As you gain skill in the selection of flame size, the resultant heating time will become minimal. Jewelers call the small pieces of solder "paillons," and each paillon should be bent in a

slightly twisted or "u" shape and placed on the pick body between. This will elevate the brass above the surface, and when the solder melts, it will let the brass slam down onto the pick for a firmer joint, which also lets you know when the solder has melted, since you cannot see it flow except at the very edge. It is possible to feed the solder in, as soft solderers are familiar with, but this is not as workmanlike as the paillon-placement method. Make sure the brass and the steel contact at all points on their faces. If the brass is bent away at all, the joint will not be very secure. The thickness of the solder film is less than .002", and the solder will not bridge large gaps or flow well. This is why the surfaces must match so well.

Once the joint is prepared, flux both surfaces and the paillons, then insert the solder paillons and place the brass over them, aligning it with the scribed lines. Do not handle the paillons with bare fingers after fluxing, as that replaces grease the flux is supposed to remove. Use a pointed tool to place the paillons. Remember, the joint must also be heated quickly to prevent the flux from spending its chemical action before the solder melts. If this happens, the flux will not protect the metal and oxides will re-form, preventing solder flow. Also, the joint must not be overheated, or warping and even actual melting of the pick metal will result. A neutral or reducing flame is best for soldering. Now, I had a lot of trouble deciding which flame was neutral, reducing or oxidizing, until I read that the white-hot luminous cone you will see as you begin to add oxygen is the result of carbon particles that have insufficient air to burn. That made it clear to me. It is also stated that a tinge of yellowish blue indicates a neutral flame, best for all-around soldering. A common technique is to establish flame size with the fuel and just a touch of oxygen, then reduce the fuel until the flame begins to roar. This will be well past oxidizing into reducing, so back off the oxygen a touch and go to it. If you are insecure about your soldering technique you can use a twist of iron binding wire to help in the alignment of the parts. The preheat serves to activate the flux and equalize the heat content of both pieces being silver-soldered. Since the hilt/handle will have more mass than the pick handle, the torch flame must linger a lot longer on the hilt until it is heated to the same temp as the pick. The heat should be applied very slowly until the alcohol in the paste flux ignites and burns away. Sometimes small steam explosions from any small water content of the flux paste might even displace a free-standing paillon or the brass itself. If this happens, nudge both back into position with a soldering needle or tweezers. A soldering needle is a non-stick alloy needle set in a wooden handle. It can be used to press parts together, align objects in the flame field, and even help in drawing the line of melted silver solder down to the proper joint areas. Once the borax fuses into a glass, the heating can then be accelerated, applying the flame from the back-side, then the front-side of the pick until the brass moves as the solder melts. Do not continue to heat the joint once the solder flows. If you do, the zinc in the solder formulation will cook off and break down the strength of the join. The heat should linger for a fraction of a second only to ensure the joint, then divert the torch flame. Don't quench the handle, let it cool slowly at first.

While not impossible, it is very difficult to make a full length handle-to-pick silver solder joint with integrity, so start with just a hilt or short handle at first, and proceed as your technique improves. The larger the pick handle mass to be silver-soldered to a pick, the larger flame size needed, so gauge the heating time accurately as you work, and if it appears that the flame will take too long to heat a large handle, or may even have insufficient heat to bring the entire handle up to temperature or hold it there despite natural cool-down, then change to a larger tip size. It always pays to use the tip adequate for the job, but excessive flame splash is difficult to clean up from nickel silver, and over heat is hard to control. Over-cooked nickel silver may develop a SUB-surface fire stain that is very difficult to remove. If you have a design that is difficult to heat-sink adequately, or you generally have trouble with silver-soldering heat-annealing the pick, consider placing an intermediate piece of metal between the pick and the hilt. This intermediate piece can be silver-soldered as hot as needed, then quenched, drilled and cold-riveted directly to the pick itself, avoiding any problems. The intermediate piece may be fairly short or even longer than the original pick steel itself, but obviously it must have sufficient free surface for the riveting. It should also be of a thickness sufficient to withstand the torsional stress put on the hilt.

Make it a point to learn to silver-solder well, and your pick designs will have no practical limits.

Chapter Fifteen
Tempering Pick Steels

I've repeated often that it is MUCH better to maintain the factory-produced temper of the shim steel; that's why you always go to great lengths to wet-grind, heat-sink, and similarly prevent over-heating. Not that you can't temper; it's just much easier to avoid it unless you need or want to.

The time to learn the mysteries and way of hot steel is now. Having progressed this far, it now becomes useful to adjust the steel hardness to suit your designs. VERY experienced professionals may alter hardness to suit some specialized intended use of each of their tools, and the ability to do this dependably is a valuable technique in the locksmith's arsenal.

While the factory-supplied temper is still best for all-around pick designs, very hard tools have uses. These special-purpose tools, usually a very tiny cross-section tool that must then be harder than the average to resist bending, are prone to a short life, and ticklish to use. There is an equation for this. The harder the pick, the easier to break; the easier to break, the less lifting force that should be used; the less lifting force used, the smaller the wrench tension to be applied; the smaller the wrench tension, the harder to dope out which pin binds. The ultimate in tools demands the ultimate in technique. If you occasionally snap a brittle pick, don't be surprised. It is the true price of success.

Hardness can also be manipulated within a given tool, making some areas tough and others springy.

How is it possible to manipulate steel so that the same piece will be either hard and soft or both? It is actually quite easy to explain: the molecular makeup of steel can exist in several different phases just like water can be gaseous steam, liquid water or solid ice. Steel that has been heated to the critical cherry red heat at which the steel becomes non-magnetic and is then quenched or instantaneously cooled, undergoes a transformation that leaves the steel not only very hard, but also as brittle as glass. It is quite easy to test this. Heat a ½″ section of a length of music wire to cherry red and plunge it into ice water. Now exert some bending tension on that heated site and it should snap right off. Heat that same part but let it cool slowly, and it is soft.

The quicker the cool, the more complete the transformation and the more brittle the steel. Picks and other tools that have just been quenched preparatory to being tempered should therefore be handled with extreme care. Even a little innocently done experimental bending can snap them and right now. In fact, if the cool is too quick the steel may even snap of its own accord from internal stresses as different parts of the steel structure cool and contract at different rates. The internal stress is what causes the tendency to fracture, either at the quench or later as the steel is stressed or bent.

An old toolmaker's trick for hardening screw thread-cutting taps was to quench the red-hot tool in mercury, and in this state it was so hard the merest scratch was enough stress to turn the tap into shards. Motor oil, brine, diesel oil, water, wet sawdust, molten salt, hot sand; the kinds of quench baths are endless. The trick is to pick a bath that will not cool too fast and make unbearable stress, or too slow and not harden by causing the phase change.

The medium choice also depends very much on the cross-section or the amount of mass in the metal being quenched. A thick piece will take quicker cooling before developing stress because the mass of the metal slows down the cooling rate. A very thin lock pick is a real challenge to quench without causing too-rapid cooling rates. Remember that fast cooling may lead to spontaneous fracturing, and too slow cooling will not produce the tempering effect. For a thin lock pick you usually cool it too quickly, so a slow bath is better.

Now that you're learning to temper your steels, it's easy to fix a too-soft pick by reheating and requenching, but a stressed pick will break and it's back to the layout process. While on this subject, let me also say that even a short period between the cherry-red heat and the quench, like for a walk across the shop or to answer a question, may spoil the quench by lowering the critical temperature below where phase change occurs, thus producing inferior results. If steel is heated to critical, but allowed to cool slowly, it stays as soft as ever. Commercial furnaces for heat-treating (tempering) often have an actual trap door to allow rapid transition from the furnace to the cooling bath beneath. The locksmith can emulate this by keeping torch, quench bath and magnet all in a 4″ radius, and shoving the correctly heated tool into the bath with all the speed of a swooping investment banker.

Of the many different cooling mediums that are used, again dependent on the cross-section or mass of the steel being quenched, plain old motor oil seems to work well for picks. For a faster, surer quench try brine water, and just live with the occasional fractured tool. Some of the tempering will be on tension wrenches, as well as picks. For the occasional pick-shank work, stick to brine. Olive oil as used in cooking also will work in place of the motor oil.

Let's assume you have just bent a pick-clothing spring to its desired contour, and now you need to reharden and temper it. A handy set up for tempering on the workbench is a steel pan filled with pea stone size pieces of pumice or a bath of clean beach sand, a stacked-up niche of firebricks, or a non-asbestos-type soldering block. All of these will reflect torch heat back up to whatever tool is placed on them for heating, and a very even temperature results. A can filled with oil or brine is placed right next to the reflecting bed, and BETWEEN the torch operator and the bed. You will also need pliers to hold the clip, and a large magnet, something with a lot of weight.

Grab a cake of high quality soap and smear it all over the clip. This will protect the surface from excessive scale formation. The scale I am referring to is a surface oxidation that develops on the steel when it is heated. The steel will chemically unite with

oxygen in the air, and the soap film retards this reaction. Light the torch and adjust it for a neutral flame, and hold the clip in the flame. As the clip becomes progressively hotter, test its attraction to the magnet. At the exact temperature when phase transformation takes place, the magnet will no longer react to the clip. Magnets do not attract steel when it is in that phase. This is called variously the critical heat and the point of decalescence. With a swift motion plunge the clip perpendicularly into the water and swirl it around a little under the water. Remove and lightly dry the clip, then carefully polish the underside of it to a brightness, using a piece torn from the roll of emery cloth. This bright spot will allow the oxidation colors to show clearly while tempering proceeds, which should be immediately after polishing. The sooner the temper is done, the more accurate the tempering will be.

Tempering is where you destroy most of the hardness you just put into your tool. A very brittle tool will snap at the slightest stressing, so you want it to be just a little bit less hard. You do that by slowly heating the tool. This is called tempering. You can gauge very accurately how the temperature is increasing by observing the colors that will bloom into the polished area of the steel. Each color indicates a level of heat, and it is usual to speak of metal being tempered (also called drawn) to a blue color or a light straw color. This tells how much of the hardness was left, and how much brittleness was removed.

Tempering is matching the brittle/soft ration of the tool to the job it's intended for. Screwdriver tips, for example, are tempered to a different color than steel cold-chisels or hacksaw blades. Experience will teach you how brittle you may leave your lock picks and still have them work dependably for your lock-opening technique.

With the same torch flame (neutral), very slowly and very evenly heat the clip until a straw color appears at the rivet end. You may frequently remove the flame from the clip to allow the heat to soak in and distribute evenly. Dip this end slightly in water now to arrest further tempering (further softening). Return the clip to the brick and reapply the flame, concentrating more on the curved area, and temper it to a blue color, then re-plunge in the water. This water quench does NOT reharden the steel, because it is not occurring from that different phase. It merely stops the heat from bleeding into areas where it is not wanted. It also halts the steel from proceeding to a softer state when the hardness required has been reached.

To recap, once the steel has been quench-hardened what this further heat-treating does is to begin to reverse the transformation back to the softer steel. The progress you allow along the road from dead brittle to dead soft determines the final degree of toughness of the steel.

Now that you have learned to temper on easy parts, you can try for the slightly tricky pick-shank procedure. Suppose you have a tool that has been heat-splashed in the critical shank region, and the dreaded bloom of blue has developed. A pick like this is unusable since it will easily bend in the region where the blue oxidation spectrum is, and must be re-hardened to be of any future use. Place the tool on the block and dim the shop lights. The subdued light allows you to gauge more accurately the energy of the glow from the heated steel. Bright room light will distort and alter the actual steel temperature colors.

Light the torch, and adjust to a neutral flame. Begin the preheat by moving the flame in a walking figure eight over the pick shank. The heat can build up excessively at the tip of the tool, much in the same way it does during a water grind, so cut the torch pattern shorter at that end. Experience will soon teach you what area will produce the desired results. After the preheat, which may take a minute or more, it's only 20–30 seconds until the steel develops the oxidation bloom. Continued heating will make the steel a dusky red, then blood red, then a color described as worm red. Testing with the magnet will show that the steel has lost its magnetic qualities where the heat is hottest at the shank. Be careful that the body of the pick, still cool enough to be magnetically attractive, does not prejudice this test. Once the critical heat has been reached, quench the pick shank perpendicularly down into the brine water. This angle of penetration ensures that no excessive warping develops, since the cooling occurs in concentric rings around the shank cross-section. If the shank breaks spontaneously, it was unavoidable. Oils are safer, but not as good. If the shank comes out intact, ver-r-ry carefully polish it with emery cloth as before and start the critical tempering process. I lay a pick flat on a rubber mat laid on the workbench to polish a brittle piece. The color to temper to is a light peacock, just barely visible as a color between violet-red and blue. Due to the extremely small cross section of the shank, the temper must be as slow as possible, since it heats up fast. I find a very small spritzer filled with water is an excellent tool to quench slightly a critical area. With this temperature control it is possible to "sculpt" the heating pattern very accurately and put the temper exactly where it is needed. Recall also that difficult heating problems may be overcome by the judicious use of a heat-sink clamp, or even touching an area desired to be cooled with a piece of steel.

Once the easier skills of pick crafting are mastered, try this demanding work of selective tempering. Some time, it may be the only technique that saves your day.

Chapter Sixteen
Lock Picks, Inc.

Eddie the wire has been all across this great land, and the lock pick seems to be close to the ultimate trade good. Everybody will show at least some interest in a set of lock pick tools, especially if they look professionally done, and not a few people are willing to spend a few dollars just to possess a set. That's reason one for having a few sets on hand to sell.

The professional lock-opener quickly finds out that having one set is just not enough. You'll need a good set for the service van, an equally good set for the shop, a starter set for your apprentice, a set to keep at home, and a set to carry with you at all times. John Bianci, the famous leather holster maker, publishes a great pair of photos in his book. The first shows him in suit and tie, absolutely normal appearing, but in the next photo his jacket is gone, pants legs up, and you can easily count over twenty guns scattered in various hideout holsters on his person.

Paradoxically, his point (called Bianci's Law) is "one gun, one carry." That means find the one combination of holster and pistol you are most suited to physically, and which most meets your needs, and learn to function with this gun and this carry. It is more efficient than changing off and never developing an instinctive "feel" for your armament.

The flip side of this is Wire's Law, which states, "you can never have too many lock picks stashed away." As I sit here writing this chapter, I have twelve tools in my wallet, my tool case, and my keychain combined. Should one break or get misplaced, I have a backup. This is reason too why you should have extra sets.

The title of this chapter, however, is Lock Picks, Inc. Always carry a simple set to sell to the average guy. You and I both know just buying the tools will not make him a lock ace overnight. In fact I hope whoever buys them will go right out and buy eddie's *Complete Guide to Lock Picking* and really learn the correct way to use the tools, but at least you can make some coin on the deal up front.

Let's get a repeat of some helpful hints here: *Possession of lock picking or other related burglary tools is a felony in many legal jurisdictions.* A case of intent can easily be built up unless you can cough up an ALOA or similar professional organization document really quickly. If you like to get attention by flashing lock picking tools in the local bar, you may get your wish. On the other hand, a one-to-one deal for a small set is worth about thirty or forty extra dollars in hand. The supply houses offer smaller sets of poorer quality steel for more money. Beating this is called enterprise. A sales formula that never fails is to demonstrate how easy it is to pop a low tolerance disc lock, and then get the potential buyer to try the same. Most anyone can rake open such a lock with a little help on the tension wrench. Once your mark has that first successful B&E under the belt, they are only too eager to buy a set of tools. In fact, you will find it's almost impossible to get someone to let go of the lock pick once they experience the almost inexpressible feeling of a lock magically opening without the key. Your customer will be shy about revealing his contact too, so you will have a loyal following.

Part of the mystique behind such a sale is indeed that admonition: "Don't tell anyone where you got these special lock picks." I can't begin to count the number of sets floating around that started on my workbench. By the way, if eddie takes a liking to you he usually gives you a set at no charge. Maybe he'll see you some where, some day. It could happen!

To be in the business in a big way, you must learn to work quickly and a little cheaply, and a set of helper tools called jigs will increase your pick per hour rate lots. Here's how.

Material selection is critical. Regular ½″ shim stock is of course best for the serious tool, but amateurs could get by with the steel used in the do-it-yourself sewer snakes found at Wal-Mart and similar emporiums. This steel is only ¼″ wide and, of course, comes on a reel. It is also blued to begin with. The first step is cutting off lengths.

Figure 55 shows the jig used for length cutting from the reel. Blanks should be 5-6″. Push the steel in until it bottoms, then hold the clamp arm down and begin to cut on the wheel edge. When the cut is a little more than halfway through in thickness, a quick jerk of the bending arm will snap it off. Experience will soon tell you when. Since you're wearing gloves it is easy to pluck out the cut piece and throw it in a tub of water. Always wear the usual eye and ear protection for such marathon work.

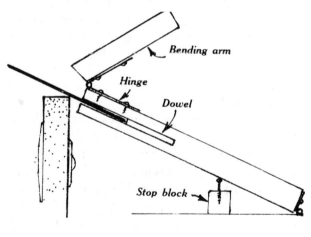

Figure 55
Mass production of wrenches.

All the pieces will have two rough-ground ends, so it won't matter which end you pick to grind the relief cut and rough tool contour on. A master pick and a scribe will make short work of generating the cut lines. If you are pack-grinding freehand, only the top pick need be marked at all. To spray all the blanks, lay them out like floor tiles on the bench, or rely on the stock blue to make layout lines appear. The object here is to save time and money.

It used to be that special gang jigs with several grinding wheels mounted side-by-side were necessary to eliminate the enormous amount of time to rough grind, and the heat build-up was so intense that cooling was a real chore. With the advent of the mist coolant system, however, pack-grinding (one marked pick on top and two or three blanks below) can now be done freehand and in record time. You can use a machinist's clamp or filament tape to bind the pack together at first, but as experience grows you will learn just to grip them tightly, and frequently slam the entire pack bottom edge down on a flat surface. This action throws all of the blanks in the pack down straight with each other if they have slipped out of line, and gives your hand time to relax.

Okay, if you are really good with the wheel the picks are rough ground to profile and need only a little polishing to sell. For production picks you must omit the nice steps of filing and/or stoning and polishing because of the hand work involved. The easy answer is to tumble the picks. Rock hounds are familiar with the rubber-lined canisters mounted on rollers motorized to turn at about 1 r.p.m. every 2-3 seconds. The barrels are usually filled with a mix of rocks and polishing media. Media can be anything from sand to corncobs and rouge to ceramic bits and pieces. Sometimes water, oil or other exotics are added as well. To use this system one merely charges the barrel, turns it on, and goes to several movies. In fact, polishing can take 2-3 days, but who cares? Eddie uses an industry media concoction called "stones and oil mod three." The oil is 20-weight motor oil, and the stones can be anything from pea gravel to sharp silica sand used by sandblasters. If you are frequenting a jewelers' supply it will have many types of media to choose from and a different type may suit you better. The key is never to tumble roughed-out picks dry, always use oil of some sort. Kerosene works, but it's a fire hazard and will swell the rubber in the barrel. Water will rust out the stock in no time. Motor oil is a good compromise. Scratching of the picks may result with this tumbling process, but it's easy and hands-off fun. Reloaders will also be familiar with the vibratory bowl method, but eddie has never tried it, so he can't say if it works.

If you don't want to invest in a commercial barrel rig, an empty one-gallon paint can works just as well (by the way, only fill the barrel ½ to ⅔ full), and a rotating cradle can easily be devised. Figure 56 shows a cradle capable of processing four cans at once, each barrel containing a different grit size charge. This is real high production. To sieve out the tools once polished, try a kitchen colander and a plastic pail. A fry basket also works. If you transfer tools from one grit to the next, wash them in between with soapy water that is VERY hot to prevent rusting.

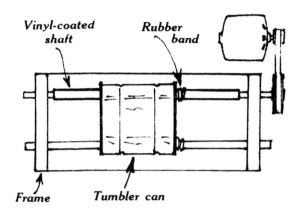

Figure 56
Polishing tumbler to finish pick steel.

This same tumble finishing works well with Formica handle blanks, which is the recommended handle material for production picks. The media here must be run dry, and be very fine to begin with. I use fine silica.

Lock pick cases present a problem, but I recommend a bank bag case with a Formica insert. The bank bags are vinyl with a coil zipper and usually available for a dollar or so from your bank. They are for big cash deposits, kind of like the establishment adult's version of the old plastic pencil case. Hilariously, although they weigh a few ounces and are 4x10 inches, they come with locks on the zippers. It is even possible to get them custom screened for a small set-up fee. Overruns are available inexpensively from the same bag companies, or right from the bank. Stress up front that you want them supplied empty, and are willing to pay for them. It saves embarrassment.

The lettering may come off with a soft scrub dipped in methylene chloride (real nasty stuff, take all precautions necessary), or it may not. The Formica insert holds the tools inserted in elastic cord loops laced through a pattern of holes in the Formica. The Formica blanks can be gang drilled for holes in large stacks.

For those of you making lock picks inside pen sets (a fountain pen with the insides gutted out and a tiny lock pick inserted), the epoxy resins are just the thing to set the pick into the pen top. These sell pretty well and eliminate finishing and... er... handling charges.

Figure 57
A professional lock tool set with a "wallet-type" carrying case.

Simple instruction sheets are a nice professional touch, and any high-powered copy shop will let you rent computer time to make laser copies of same. Consult a local users' group in your flavor of computer for lots of friendly advice about which software to get for writing and so on. If you can obtain access to a high-resolution flatbed scanner, you can keep a running file of all your pick designs. Just lay them all out on the scanner's glass and make the scan at the highest resolution possible. The resulting image may then be reprinted, altered in a variety of ways to make the edges more distinct, or the edges themselves may even be altered very precisely using a graphics program that is "zoomed-in" very tightly. At 1200 DPI, subtle changes in the contour of any lock pick are a snap. Once the pick is altered, a laser printout can be saturated with rubber cement and applied directly to a steel blank for grinding. Eddie uses a Microtek scanner wired to a Macintosh Quadra 610 with Photoshop and Canvas for software. All images are bit-mapped. Once the picks have been digitized they can also be filed and cross filed in a simple flat-file database and sorted out by category, tip height, any criteria you desire. The actual high (and high-meg) file need not be filed, just a low-resolution stand-in for bookmark purposes. Most of this is foreign to you, but a user group will explain it all. In eddie's neck of the woods, Kinko's copies has all the equipment, software and expertise needed on line.

As the Coneheads would say, "This technical discourse on subject matter of mass quantities of lock manipulation devices is completed."

Chapter Seventeen
Wafer Tumbler Tools

Having progressed this far, you certainly know the main lock mechanism types: lever tumbler, plain warded, pin tumbler, disc tumbler, cylinder (ACE) tumbler, and sidebar tumbler. There are also a few oddball types like the Bell lock (1920s vintage), and one curiosity that is commonly seen, although not currently in production: the Schlage wafer tumbler lock system. Schlage had some specific design recommendations in mind when evolving the wafer tumbler; it had to be easily mass produced, yet long wearing. It had to be easily masterkeyed, while still providing enough of a security leap over the common disc tumbler, since it was slated to be used primarily for the residential duty exterior lockset market. They achieved this added security (so they thought) by using eight wafer positions in each lockset instead of the usual four or five per disc tumbler locks. This lock system is further unusual in that both keycuts and a lack of keycuts cooperate to align tumblers at the shear line. The key is two-sided and each side is independent in its bitting of the other side. Furthermore, there are only two depths of cut: either cut .060″ deep or not cut at all. Such systems exist in some European locks as well. All of the eight tumbler positions can have combination tumblers inserted right side up or upside down so that tumblers have two possible orientations in the lock, to which the key bitting must match. We are not talking about two different tumblers per position. Only one fits, but it can be inserted either regular or flipped over.

We will not concentrate on the specific mechanics of the lock here. First of all, the tool you will use to open these locks requires no skill in manipulation, so it's not necessary to know precisely how it works. If you want more detailed knowledge, if you're curious about how this tool works, just pick up a lock of this type and play around with it. The operation is easily understood with the lock actually in hand.

There are three variations of keyway profile, but one is a master-key type seldom seen. The two common keyways each require a tool that is fitted to them, and each of the keyways has an "A" or a "B" flavor that is really not keyway-related but due to an item called the master wafer. The master wafer is the furthest tumbler inside the lock, and at rest it protrudes out from the cylinder. It is pushed in to align at shear by the absence of a cut on the far end of the key. The master wafer may also be reversed or flipped in the lock, and the lack of cut will then have to be on the reverse side of the key, hence the "A" or "B" flavor of the lock. The side opposite this uncut portion of the key must, however, be cut to allow the key to be fully inserted in the lock. Carefully note that the key can only be inserted one way, and cannot be turned and inserted 180 degrees. This is due to the keyway warding (really, the keyway shape). Consequently, you cannot flip your tool over if the master wafer cut is on the wrong side. You will need two tools, an "A" and a "B," for each of the two keyway variations, or four tools in all.

The master wafer (the farthest from the keyway opening) is followed by a random selection of two other wafer types: series wafers and combination wafers. These fill up all the rest of the slots available. The series wafers function just like the master wafer; they require an uncut portion of key to push or retract them into the cylinder and align them at shear, but they cannot be flipped. The combination wafers are normally inside the cylinder, and any uncut portion of key will cause them to protrude and misalign with the shear line. Consequently, the combination wafers require key cuts to keep from being forced out of shear, and the series wafers require no cuts since a cut will unalign shear. When a lock is set up to a given keycode, the locksmith proceeds by putting a combination wafer into each of the fourteen position/orientation slots remaining which are designated in the coding system, and then filling the remainder of the slots with series wafers. All together there are eight slots with tumblers either inserted up or down, so there are 16 possibles. A combination tumbler may protrude from either side of the cylinder, a series only from one side. It sounds confusing, but I told you that no theory is really required to do these locks. The only real quirk of this lock is the combination wafer, which will lock if you touch or disturb it. Other than that, this is a lock that will unlock if you fully lift all the series and master wafers. It's really simple.

If you follow this discussion it is easy to see that the security of this locking system is zip except for the series wafers which keep the cylinder locked while at rest. All that is required to fox this lock is to identify mechanically which are the combination wafers and leave them alone, while raising all the series and master wafers to shear while exerting torque on the cylinder to create the usual "lip." When all the series and the correct master wafer are at shear the lock snaps open.

To bypass these locks easily, it is possible to cut a very special set of four keys that will do most of the work for you. This key set is produced by cutting down a regular key set from a wafer lock so you will need to have one each of the two KEYWAY types in hand.

After disassembling this lock down to the core, insert the matching key and observe the reaction of each tumbler as the bitting slides by it. Eventually all the tumblers will line up to shear. The object here is to identify whether your particular key is a type one or type two. If the hollowed-out side of the key is away from you and the extreme tip cut is on the bottom half of the key, it is a type one. If on top, it's a type two. Now align a keyblank onto your key (get a keyblank for this lock at any five-and-dime), and trace all the cut troughs on the blank. Connect these troughs (full cuts) on the side of the key with the tip cut out with a straight line that runs from key tip all the way through the bow. Even the bow will be cut flush to allow room for an additional tool. The troughs that are on the NON-cut tip side are also connected, but these are

only cut as shown in Figure 58. The end result is a key that has no guts except at the tip. In other words, this key will retract only the master tumbler. Remember, the master comes in the far end position (deepest in the lock) only, and always protrudes into the lock case, locking the lock unless it is retracted by a non-cut on an inserted key. When you insert this key, then, it will retract the master and not advance or retract any other tumblers. This key must have a twin that will retract the master tumbler if it is inserted upside down, as it is designed to be. There are two tools, then: one for master up, and one for master inverted. There are two types of keyway, so those are your four key tools in all. Once produced, they should be riveted together in matching pairs in such an orientation that the probe will have unobstructed access to the flush-cut top of the key tool.

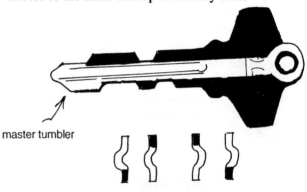

master tumbler

Figure 58
Shaded areas cut away to make master wafer pick-key.

Okay, you go to the lock, figure out which keyway it is, select the correct pair of key tools, select one and insert it. If you don't feel any contact with the master tumbler, it's the wrong tool, so insert the right one. The right one will retract the master. To complete the lock picking process, you must now retract all the series wafers to shear, and the lock will snap open. To manipulate the series wafers, insert the second tool, a slim handle-mounted probe, and use it to lift all the series wafers by pushing to the outside of the keyway (away from the keyway center). While holding all these wafers at shear, apply tension to the core using the handy fold-down other half of the key tool. After applying hard tension, withdraw the probe, and slightly relax turning tension on the core. The lock will snap.

The assumption is that a key tool is an automatic thing like a set of tryout keys. The truth is, the key tool is just a convenient way to make a tool, and some skill is still involved. It is possible to fail an opening using this system. A second try usually succeeds. With all tools, a little practice yields rich rewards. Since the Schlage is still very prevalent, it is worthwhile to make and carry a set of bypass tools as described.

Chapter Eighteen
Pick Guns

The mail order suppliers often tack on a 120% increase on prices of lock pick guns. The average guy doesn't have access to locksmith suppliers, so how do you get a pick gun? Figure 59 shows the side view of a manually operated model.

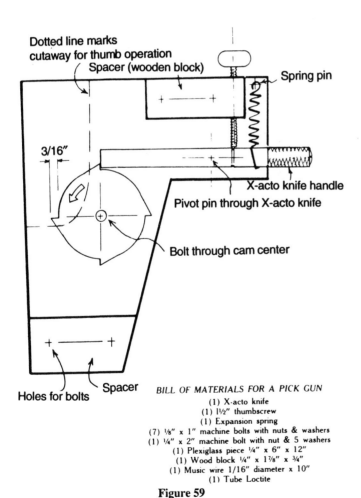

Dotted line marks
cutaway for thumb operation
Spacer (wooden block)

Spring pin

3/16″

X-acto knife handle

Pivot pin through X-acto knife

Bolt through cam center

Spacer

Holes for bolts

BILL OF MATERIALS FOR A PICK GUN
(1) X-acto knife
(1) 1½″ thumbscrew
(1) Expansion spring
(7) ⅛″ x 1″ machine bolts with nuts & washers
(1) ¼″ x 2″ machine bolt with nut & 5 washers
(1) Plexiglass piece ¼″ x 6″ x 12″
(1) Wood block ¼″ x 1⅞″ x ¾″
(1) Music wire 1/16″ diameter x 10″
(1) Tube Loctite

Figure 59
Pick gun side phantom view.

Cut the two side pieces by tracing onto a piece of Masonite, heavy sheet metal, or plastic — you need two pieces. You can also photocopy the figure twice, and glue the copies onto the stock. Make sure to center-punch for all holes to be drilled. Once you have two gun halves with holes drilled, purchase the rest of the materials listed, and drill the holes in the X-acto knife handle. If you have a "V" block, that will help in getting them perfectly aligned. The next step is to cut the cam, which can be made from ¼″ thick Plexiglas or plywood or Masonite. I prefer the plastic. The needles that chuck into the knife can be cut from extra length blades that fit the knife — just grind the blade down to a straight tool like your feeler pick.

The next step is to begin assembly by threading a washer on the cam bolt, putting this assembly through one gun half, then a nut locked on with Loctite (a compound that permanently "freezes" threads in position). Now coat both cam and nut with contact cement and install the cam, then a washer, then the other gun half, then a washer and a nut with more Loctite. Into this assembly, install the X-acto knife, the blocks for the spring and stop mechanisms, the spring and stop screw, and finally the crank handle.

The crank handle is bent from the music wire and is inserted into a hole drilled through the end of the cam bolt, just like the holes drilled in the X-acto handle.

Notice that the thickness of the spring and stop blocks must be adjusted with the addition of washers and paper spacers to their holding bolts to ensure no warping strain is put on the gun. Once all the other bolts are installed and Loctited, regulation is next. (Note: Loctite and its releasing compound are available in most cycle supply shops. Because of the vibration of both cycles and lock pick guns, it is necessary for all bolts that may work loose.)

Regulation is accomplished by inserting a small strip of paper between the cam and knife handle where it bears on the cam. Turn the stop screw until the paper is just free. This ensures that the screw, not the cam face, takes all of the jar of the knife handle as it snaps up. This adjustment should be periodically repeated as the gun "settles."

Now adjust the spring to provide slight tension with the knife in the rest position (on the stop screw). You may want to vary the spring tension as you work the gun to provide different results. It all depends on your style and the lock in question. Generally, more tension is more controllable, though.

In use, the needle is clamped in the chuck, and then a moderate-weight tension wrench is inserted in the keyway. (See Chapter Eleven for weighted tension wrenches.) Then the needle is pushed in straight under all the pins, and the operator turns the crank with a steady speed. The cam alternately pushes and releases the knife, and the spring tension is transmitted via the knife and needle to the bottom pins, which in turn slam the top pins up. At some point, there is a gap between both sets of pins, and the tension weight turns the core, opening the lock. Varying cranking speed may help. Another possible variation is to turn the stop screw in even more, which will reduce the travel of the needle, but more travel is usually better. Heavy tension on the core is definitely to be avoided.

If you feel that you must have hand control of the tension wrench, your gun can be modified by cutting away the rear portion, exposing the outer perimeter of the cam for a least 120° sector of travel. Then you can use the holding hand thumb to actuate the cam surface with one hand free for the tension wrench. A real enthusiast could convert this gun to clockwork or electrical operation, allowing you to be elsewhere if necessary while the gun operates — but that is a little too much "James Bond" for me.

Chapter Nineteen
A Tool for Picking Tubular Locks

Eddie does it again! Lock tools to pick tubular locks are always expensive and hardly ever mentioned. Let's build one for five dollars.

First, are you up on elementary tubular lock theory? These locks are the kind with circular keyholes that show up on vending machines. Close examination shows that the pin tumbler principle is used, but the pins are placed end-forward in a circle. The outer portion is fixed, and holds the top pins in the bottom. The inner portion is movable, rotates around a center fastened to the outer portion (at the bottom), and holds the bottom pins whose ends you see in the keyway.

In operation, the tubular key is inserted to fit over the inner post (inner portion), and a lug protruding from the key fits into a slot cut in both inner and outer portions of the lock.

The key is then pressed in, and while the outer lug clears the slot, the inner one stays bearing on the groove cut for it in the movable portion. Simultaneously, different depth cuts on the edge of the key (corresponding to bitting on a regular key) push in the bottom pins to their respective shearlines. Once shear is reached, the inner portion can be turned, and it is the inner lug of the key riding on the slot that does the turning. If this is a little unclear, it is because I am trying to condense. Get a tubular lock and study it to be sure you understand this theory.

The most important thing to remember in all this is that unlike a pin tumbler lock where the bottom pins are trapped and perform no further function as the core is rotated, in the tubular lock the bottom pins must be held at shear line continually, or when the lock inner portion rotates over exactly one pin hole, the top pin will snap into the hole and relock the tubular lock. Therefore, even if you were to pick each

pin stack individually and begin rotation of the core (inner portion), the entire set of pin stacks would relock as the next pin hole came up. Theoretically, you would need to repick each pin stack eight times to get one complete rotation. Furthermore, since many of the locks are in applications where nine or ten turns are needed to unscrew the locking mechanism fully, the individual pick artist can be in real trouble. That is why tubular lock picks are configured as shown in Figure 60.

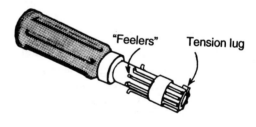

Figure 60
Commercially produced tubular lock pick,
showing "feeler" picks.

In practice, the operator puts tension on the core via the lug protruding from the inner face of the tube. Once tension is applied, the operator begins to exert a wiggling downward push on the tool, and its eight fingers begin to push each pin end simultaneously, driving them all to the shear line. The amount of pressure each feeler exerts on the pin stacks is adjusted by adding or removing turns from the rubber band around the feelers and rod. It must be enough to counteract the opposite push of the pin springs, but not so much that it pushes the pins past shear. This pressure is the analog to lifting pressure with the regular lock pick.

To begin producing the pick, purchase a tubular lock — regular eight pin with center keyway (the most common) — to use as a gauge for buying brass tubing. You need one piece that snugly fits over the inner portion just like the key, and the next telescoping size smaller. You also need a length of music wire one-sixteenth inch in diameter and 36 inches long, and a 20 inch piece of brass tubing that the wire telescope fits into.

These materials with telescope fit can be purchased at hobby stores that sell to model airplane hobbyists. Begin by cutting a piece of the music wire, bending it double, and using epoxy or super-glue to attach it to the edge of the tube fitting over the lock's inner portion (called a nose). Make sure that the wire extends the full depth of the lock on the inside tube edge, and only half that outside.

This will be the lug that engages the groove to put tension on the nose. When the glue is dry, cut the tube exactly double the length that it bottoms in the lock. It should protrude the same amount outside of the lock as it goes in. Also cut the other, smaller tube to a four inch length. Cutting both tubes requires finesse and a fine-toothed hacksaw. Go slowly and try to avoid bending the tube. When finished, carefully de-burr the end and file square if you goofed and cut it on an angle. The tubes *must* be flat and square. Leave yourself a little over-length if necessary.

Now slip the two tubes together, insert this assembly into the lock, bottom both tubes, and mark the point where the larger tube and the smaller tube meet by scribing a line on the smaller tube. Remove the assembly, spread superglue or epoxy on the join and re-join the tubes, using the scribed line to position the two properly. Tape them together in this relationship and let dry.

Now comes the hard part. You need to cut eight lengths of the smallest brass tube, and eight lengths of the music wire that telescope into the tube. Each tube should be 1½ inches long. The music wire segments should be 2¼ inches long. Be very careful when cutting the tubing, as the wire must later slide freely inside it.

When the tubes and wires are all cut and deburred, insert the dry, glued tube assembly (large tubes) into the lock and run tape from the end of the tube to the sides of the lock, effectively pushing it into the lock. Now spread some very thick epoxy glue onto the first inch and a half of the large tube assembly above the lock face. Only apply the glue to the area where one of the small tubes will stick.

Now apply one of the tubes pointing exactly in line with the pin tumbler axis. If necessary, slide a piece of music wire inside the tube and down to the pin to precisely align the tube. Once it is roughly aligned, put tape around the assembly to hold the small tube in place. Let dry. Do this entire procedure for each of the other seven tubes, and be sure to align each one in turn precisely. If even one is canted and not parallel with the pin tumbler axis, excessive friction will result as the pick is operated.

Once all eight are mounted and dry, insert one of the music wire rods into the tube and see if it will clear the inside rim of the lock and contact the pin end. If it will, fine. If not (this may vary with different locks), grind a flat on each rod until they will all clear to contact the pin end and not touch the rim. The flat must extend up far enough on the rod to allow the rod to bottom the pin. Remember to touch up the grind a little with a file to prevent metal slivers from jamming the lock.

The final step is to insert all the rods into their respective tubes, and put a doubled and tripled rubber band around the whole assembly to hold the rods.

Chapter Twenty
The Plug Spinner

The next professional lock tool is something every pick expert should carry. Occasionally you will succeed in picking a lock only to find that you are on the locked side of turning, and if you reverse the turning towards unlocking, the pins will fall back into the holes, and you must start over. However, a plug spinner applies a sudden forceful rotation to the plug and, by applying a centrifugal force to the pins, bypasses the locked position and unlocks the plug.

You need the following materials:

One piece ¼″ diameter music wire *(for shank)*

One piece .030″ diameter music wire, 18 inches long *(for spring)*

One piece of tubing that slips over the above music wire (the fit should be precise)

One flat stock, brass or aluminum, 1½″ x 10 inches x one-thirty-second inch (these dimensions are approximate)

One machine screw ¼″ x ¾″, with two washers and a nut

One flat stock 1½″ x 4 inches x one-thirty-second inch

Start by grinding two parallel flats 1″ long on one end of the ten inch piece of ¼″ o.d. music wire. This is the same cut that you make for tension wrenches. Cut until a thin blade is formed that will fit in a keyway. Now drill a one-sixteenth inch diameter hole in the middle of the blade as shown in Figure 61. Finally, bend one inch of the other end into a right angle and then another one inch section back again, forming a crank. A vise and hammer may be necessary for the bending. That wire is tough! Next cut a piece of tubing as long as the flat stock is wide, and set it aside. The next step is to form the flat stock

around the music wire. Try to follow the curve of the wire as much as possible — a pair of pliers may help to do this. After the stock has been formed, remove the wire, thread the tubing section onto the end and form the flat stock over the tubing/wire combination. Now place one of the washers on the flat stock so that the top edge just touches where the stock starts to curve. Hold the washer in this position, and mark the center for drilling a hole. Now remove the washer and drill the hole, then put a washer on the bolt, and finally the nut. Tighten this assembly, but check for rotation of the music wire. Do not crush the tube.

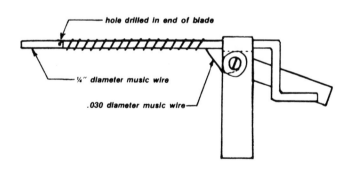

Figure 61
Shop-built plug spinner.

The next step is to insert one end of the .030″ music wire in the hole drilled in the ¼″ music wire, and bend it back around the .030″ wire, locking the end. Now use your fingers to guide the wire about the ¼″ shaft, while you turn the crank end. You are in effect winding a spiral spring up to the flat stock handle. Leave about two inches of wire and wrap a loop or two around the machine bolt under the washer on the head side on the handle to anchor the other end. Finally drill a hole in the 1½″ x 4″ x one-thirty-second inch stock piece and put it on under the washer on the nut side to act as a trigger.

To use, first wind the crank in the opposite direction of what you want the plug to turn. When tight enough, lift up the trigger to block the crank from turning, then insert the blade in the keyway of the wrong-picked plug. Hold the tool by the handle and, watching your fingers, release the trigger. Presto! If you have trouble, try winding the spring tighter. You may also find that two tools, a lefthand and a righthand wound spring, will allow you to tighten the spring rather than winding the spring in some cases. An unwound spring does not spin as forcefully.

Chapter Twenty One
Car Opening Tools

Next, we will discuss car-opening tools. First, let me say that all of the professional lock tool/key outline tracing techniques are applicable to tools that will work non-GM locks. GM locks can only be opened by a snake pick capable of literally lining up all the tumblers simultaneously. Once the shutter over the keyway is bypassed, picking can proceed as usual. It may be useful to secure a couple of junk auto locks and grind off the front of the lock, exposing the keyway to allow for easy tool sizing. However, there is a tool that bypasses door locks only. Grind the tool shown in Figure 62 from one-sixteenth inch tempered or spring steel stock. Possible sources are hardware store stock bins, elevator bands, discarded large bandsaw blades, or metal house wind bracing. Please note: this tool is inserted between the outside weather stripping and the glass, directly above the door lock.

Figure 62
Good old slim jim

It works by hooking some of the locking mechanism inside the door, either by pulling up or pushing down. Also remember occasionally to try to open the door to see if it has been unlocked yet. This tool works on all cars, all years, except those which have metal boxes protecting the locking mechanism.

The Slim Jim

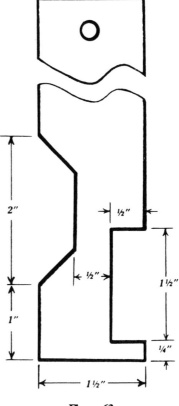

Figure 63
Slim Jim end detail.

The next subject to cover is the slim jim. Instructions (brief) on manufacture and use of a slim-jim were given in the first edition of *How To Make Your Own Professional Lock Tools, Volume Two* but a new and better model is currently in use. In fact, a recent publication lists six versions of this tool, plus a Corvette-opening tool. My tool is cut from an aluminum shop ruler, available at most hardware stores. The ruler I use is three feet long and one and one half inches wide. Cut a twenty-three inch long piece with a hacksaw, and grind the end as shown in Figure 63.

The measurements are given so that you can spray with toolmaker's ink and scribe the pattern on the ruler directly. With the right lighting, you can even omit the toolmaker's ink. These rulers are all tempered aluminum, so watch for heat build-up as usual, and quench frequently. If your first stop is an art store, look for a flexible tempered steel ruler in a length that is close to twenty three inches, and use it instead.

Now that the end has been cut to profile, the thickness of the working end must be specially sharpened to avoid catching on the weather stripping on all car windows.

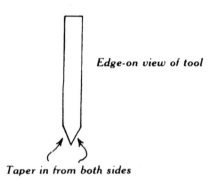

Edge-on view of tool

Taper in from both sides

Figure 64
Edge-on view of slim jim.

Figure 64 shows the profile for sharpening. It allows two-way tool insertion and no hang-ups. A hole should also be drilled in the handle end of the tool, one-eighth inch in diameter and located a quarter of an inch from the edge. Finally, get a large heavy rubber band and double it around the shank of the tool. Working the tool is fairly simple. Simply insert the working end between the weather stripping and the glass at the driver's or passenger's side, straight down from where the lock cylinder is. Disregard where the inside button is. The object is to hook either the camming mechanism or linkage that is attached to the back of the lock cylinder, or hook the rocker shaped latch assembly located at the back edge of the door. Once hooked, a simple pull, or alternately, a push down, will unlock the door.

There are finer points, though. One is to lubricate the weather stripping with a spray silicone or hand cream for easier insertion. Some cars, notably Fords, have two layers of stripping — in this case, go through the middle. A fifteen to twenty five degree bend in the

tool end may be very helpful in contacting the lock mechanism — once you get it right, keep it bent. Occasionally, while working the tool, the door unlocks but does not open, so try the button on the handle once or twice while working, and watch the inside button.

Another point is that smaller cars, especially of foreign manufacture, will have bolts that obstruct the straight down maneuver, but an angling movement will avoid these. Some cars even open with a sideways push on the tool shank.

Now to the rubber band. Before insertion in the door, hold the tool with the hook on the cylinder and slide the rubber band until it is level with the top of the door. This will provide an accurate measure of how far down to insert the tool. In fact, if the inch markings are intact on the ruler, you can go by those and save the extra time involved in rubber banding. After all, time is of the essence while opening.

I strongly advise that you keep records of each attempted opening so that you can duplicate it next time. Some people keep a notebook listing make, model and comments.

Some makes and models of cars from 1979 on have metal shields or framing members that impede this slim jim. For those tricky situations, I recommend a length of three thirty-seconds of an inch diameter music wire with a handle looped in one end and a right angle bend on the other end.

The right-angle member should be an inch and a quarter long, and the whole tool should be twenty three inches. This tool is inserted by putting the end of the bend straight down through the weather stripping (a little sharpening may be helpful here in avoiding metal retainer clips — but not too sharp) then bringing the shank of the tool up ninety degrees to normal working position. This puts the right angle bend inside the door with a minimum of forcing. From there the tool can be used as normal, although it will have a tendency to hang up easily. When that occurs, don't panic, just work the tool back and forth slowly and it will free up.

A rubber band on the shank of this tool is very helpful in locating the locking mechanism depth properly. The hole on the other end can be used as a lasso to open mushroom style inside knobs, the threaded wire that remains when the knob is removed, and some types of anti-theft smooth knobs. Just bend at an angle and insert; as the tool is pulled over the knob it will cant and dig into the surface, pulling up the knob.

Another well-known (to most people I know, anyway) dodge is tying some fishing line to the hole, then leading the end back through, up the tool shank, and out the car. The noose that results can be looped over a button and tightened by a pull on the line, then the whole tool pulled to lift the bottom. Oh, by the way, avoid all of the other car opening tools on the market. Most of them are designed to operate the inside button, and only the slim jim is truly reliable.

Chapter Twenty Two
The Pin Tumbler Simulator

This tool alone is worth more than the price of this book. The pin tumbler simulator gives instant and visual feedback as to the exact position of the pick tip and shank while in the lock. It is invaluable for practice.

If you don't already have a cheap five-pin tumbler lock in your collection, get one. Try to get one that has a spring retainer that can be easily removed, like a clip. (Note: if you don't know what I'm talking about, please refer to *The Complete Guide to Lock Picking*.)

To prepare the lock, have five letter envelopes ready. Insert the key and turn the plug 90°. Hold the lock upright and remove the spring well retainer, allowing the springs to release tension gradually. With fingers or tweezers, remove the five springs and place in one envelope. Now hold your finger over the spring well holes, invert the lock, and uncover one hole at a time, dropping each top pin into a different envelope. Label the envelopes. Now tape the plug in its 90° position and set aside.

The diameter of the pins should be .115 inches, but there are variations. You need five pieces of rod as close to the pin diameter as possible, and at least four inches long. Possible sources include:

- Drill rod (at industrial supply or machine shop supply stores)
- Regular drills (wood or metal twist)
- Music wire (the old standby, but hard to get exact diameters)
- Nails (usually 16 d)
- Welding rod
- Any metal rod that will fit with *precision*. (A sloppy fit will greatly degrade the simulator's performance.)

If you don't have measuring equipment (a micrometer is best) take along the taped lock casing and use it as a fit gauge. Drill rod and drills will probably be the easiest choice. With the drill rod you may buy a long piece and grind off appropriate lengths. In fact, once you have the rod, grind one end (the non-spiral end on a drill) perfectly flat, to mate with the bottom pins in the lock.

Next, the lock must be mounted. It can be clamped in a vise, or a "C" clamp. If it is a rim cylinder, the mounting hardware it came with can be used. Just get a board 4″ x 4″ x ½″ (dimensions not critical) and drill two holes through it to screw the lock end first to the board. See Figure 65.

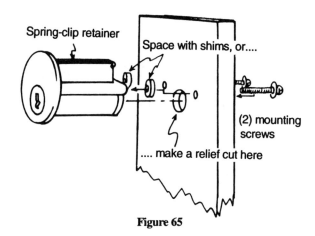

Spring-clip retainer

Space with shims, or....

(2) mounting screws

.... make a relief cut here

Figure 65

If needed, the board can be cut away slightly to allow the plug end to rotate freely, or the lock can be spaced from the board with washers or paper shims. This board can in turn be vise-clamped, or screwed to any vertical surface, even your regular practice board (see *The Complete Guide To Lock Picking*).

If the lock is a mortise type, get a board 4″ x 8″ x ½″ and cut or drill in the exact center a hole the same diameter as the lock. Next, saw the board at the middle of the hole and get two pieces 4″ x 4″ with a half-circle in the top. Glue and nail these together and glue the lock in the half-circle with contact cement. See Figure 66.

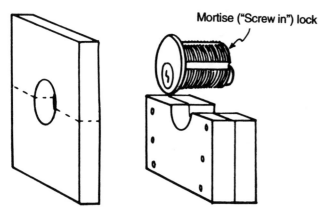

Figure 66

Mount as before. After mounting is completed, untape and return the plug to full-up position. Note that five bottom pins are now laying in the pin wells, held in by gravity. Place one prepared rod in each of the five holes, making sure that they bottom. Wiggling the plug may help, and be sure the rod has no burrs or grinding sprue to impede fit or jam the lock.

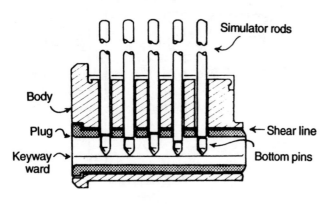

Figure 67
Practice simulator.

Once the rods are seated, put a drop of oil in each pin hole. The simulator is now complete — how does it operate? Insert the individually-lifting pick in the keyway and attempt to lift each rod in turn from front to back. Notice that the weight of the top rod simulates the spring tension as normal. If the weight of the rod seems excessive, cut or grind off a little from the *top* of the rod. Also notice that if the shank of the pick contacts a

pin stack (a real no-no) the simulator will show it. This lock can be picked as usual (concentrate on individually lifting techniques). When working the lock, keep your eye on all the rods. Remember that gravity alone holds the lock together. For transport, tape all the rods down securely. See Figure 67.

The concept can also be applied to the lever lock. Obtain a lever lock with three or four levers and a small case. Carefully grind off the top of the case, allowing top access to the levers. Now get some clear celluloid, plastic, or paper. It should be as rigid, and as thin, as possible. Fit a flag cut from the stock so that it is glued to the *face* of one of the lever tumblers, and protrudes from the top of the case (ground off).

Cut this flag until it fits properly and then use it as a pattern for the others. It may be necessary to cut tiny washers from the same material to thread over the pivot post that the tumblers are on, in order to "space" tumblers. If this is done it will prevent the levers from binding against each other due to the increased thickness caused by the flags. Experimentation will determine where to put the washers. See Figure 68.

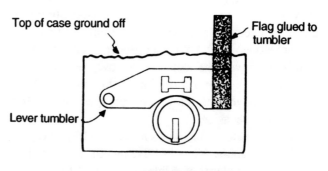

Figure 68
Front view of lever lock simulator.

Once all of the flags have been cut and applied (use contact cement), the lock should be reassembled (with washers, if necessary) and then the flags should be cut off flush with each other about a half inch above the case. Trim them to the same height *only* with the proper key inserted and turned to the top dead center position. This means that when the tumblers are next aligned so as to unlock the bolt, their tops will all be at the same height. Obviously, if a tumbler has been over-lifted (a real problem) it will also show up. This system can be further improved by color-coding the flags, and also by providing a "standard" flag attached to the case that never varies in height. With paper flags this is especially important. See Figure 69.

Professional lock experts will greatly appreciate this simulator because lever locks are the hardest to practice individually lifting techniques on, yet their use is widespread in high-security applications, such as mail and security boxes.

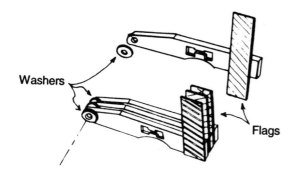

Figure 69
Spacing washers for simulator levers
(thickness of flags/washers exaggerated).

Chapter Twenty Three
Making a Tool for Impressioning
a Lock Cylinder

The next discussion is not strictly about lock picking tools but is vitally important. Impressioning a lock cylinder will be treated it in detail here, and I will show you a tool for same. Only impressioning a pin-tumbler cylinder will be covered, because other types of locks can be easily bypassed by other techniques in less time and with less inventory. Inventory is the key work here — none of the impressioning books tell you that a set of fifty or sixty blanks is required to impression an unknown lock effectively. Some keyways (notably hotels, grand master systems, and government installations) are unavailable in blank form. Nevertheless, let's look into the technique.

When you insert the proper key in a pin-tumbler lock and turn it, what prevents the key from being withdrawn during rotation? A little thought will show you that during insertion, the bottom pins were pushed up past the shearline of the plug and into the top pin wells by the various height key cuts. However, when the plug is rotating, there are no top pin key wells to provide a space for the bottom pins to go if the key were pulled out. So what happens is that as the attempt is made to withdraw the key, the bottom pins are wedged up by the sloping key cuts, and rise until they contact the shearline and the inner surface of the outer shell that the plug or cylinder moves in. When they contact this outer shell, they press against it and stop lifting, thereby preventing further key withdrawal. The item to note here is that they press against the top shell.

Now remember that during the usual picking process, the pin stack can be upside-down picked. That means that the pin stack is totally lifted into the top pin well, and then the stack is racked while the tension is relaxed. At some point, the pin stack will slide down until the shearline of the pin stack meets the shearline of the plug and outer shell. At that point, the bottom of the

top pin hangs up on the lip created by attempting to rotate the plug, and that stack is said to be picked.

Impressioning works both ways, taking advantage of both principles. A keyblank is inserted into the keyway and the blank is turned to bind all of the pinstacks. While still applying turning tension, the bow or head of the key is rapped lightly with a hammer, first straight up, then straight down. See Figure 70.

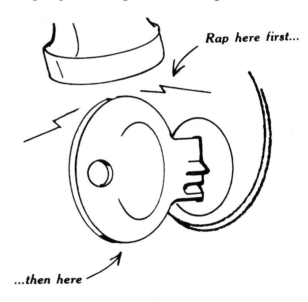

Rap here first...

...then here

Figure 70

This rapping produces marks on the keyblank top as the bound pin ends dig into the key surface. Think — they have nowhere to go when the keyblank surface comes up to meet them, so they make marks in the keyblank.

The next step is to remove the keyblank and examine it for marks. With a half-*round* file, start a keycut at each mark location. Now re-insert the key and repeat the process. A point is reached finally at which one pin stack is lifted up only to the shearline. At that point, when you insert, turn, and tap the keyblank, the top pin is held at shear and only the bottom pin riding the blank. This bottom pin alone does not make marks on the keyblank surface, so you know not to file any deeper at that spot. Eventually, all the filing will be done for each pin stack, and the cylinder will turn. Congratulations, you just made a key for that lock!

It's usually not that easy, though, but a little extra knowledge and some practice will make it that easy. First of all, selecting a key blank is important. The proliferation of key blanks on the market of various brands today makes it difficult but there are not nearly as many keyways, so stacking a set of blanks is possible. The easiest way to get a set is to make a package deal with a small key duplicator, like a dime or drug store. You many even be able to pick up an entire stock and key duplicating machine to boot. In any event, look for quality keyblanks, and try to avoid light metal alloys and aluminum blanks.

Next, be sure that the keyway is well filled, because some master key systems and some keyways vary only slightly in dimension, so avoid a lot of play in the keyblank/keyway fit. A tool that can help you a lot in impressioning is a cast metal turnbuckle fitted with a thumbscrew.

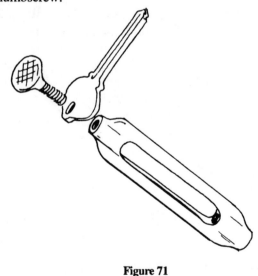

Figure 71

Any well-stocked hardware store carries turn-buckles(not the aluminum extrusion type, but cast) and a machine screw thumbscrew to match the threads of the right-hand side. Be sure not to get a thumbscrew so large in diameter that it will not fit through the smallest hole in the bow of each keyblank you stock. If so, the tool obviously cannot be used. In fact, it may be better to try for two sizes. Also, get two fender washers that are a tight fit on the thumbscrew. The selected keyblank is threaded onto the thumbscrew, using the fender washers if they will not obstruct the keyway insertion, and then firmly screwed into the turnbuckle. The left-hand threaded piece is removed. This combination provides an effective handle to apply turning tension to the keyblank, and also a filing holder. If you are improvising, a metal rod that will fit the hole is also good, but not as firm. See Figure 71

Remember when buying the turnbuckle to pick up a half-round mill file to do the key cuts with. If you wish, you can even buy a vise at some stores that is small enough to carry, or clamp to the top of your toolbox. In a field situation a "C" clamp can be used to hold the keyblank while filing — or just use any level surface. Onto the next step.

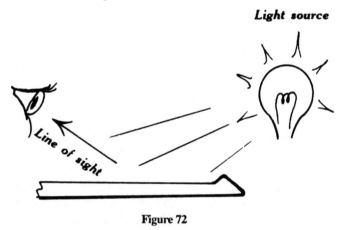

Figure 72

Before inserting the keyblank for the first impression, it is usually wise to take a flat mill file and clean off the top .002″ of an inch from the keyblank. This is necessary because the manufacturing process produces a hard skin that does not take impressions as well as the softer metal underneath. After this filing (keep the blade top square with the keyblank sides), polish the filed surface with emery cloth to remove scratches. Scratch removal is necessary because the impression the pin ends make are usually very, very faint. In fact, they are not "marks" so much as changes in the glossiness of the key finish. A number of methods all make the marks show up better — breathing on the key to deposit a thin film of moisture, using a magnifying glass, and the traditional shining a light obliquely onto the key blade. Oblique lighting (like the light of the setting sun) makes small changes in the key surface throw shadows much larger than the marks themselves, so try to master this important technique. See Figure 72. It may be essential if you work in low light conditions.

Once the initial marks have been made (you have to twist hard and also rap hard sometimes to produce a mark), some specialists like to scribe light lines on the sides of the keyblade, perpendicular to the key, that show how the cut is supposed to proceed, namely straight down. See Figure 73.

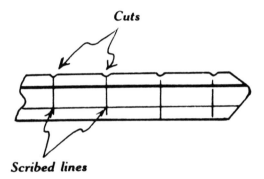

Cuts

Scribed lines

Figure 73

This has become popular, because if the cut starts to vary (and what hand filing doesn't?) from straight down, the pin will mark the side of the cut and not the bottom, making reading impossible. A small machinist's square or a depth gauge will produce the required marks. If you mark the key, remember to follow those marks strictly.

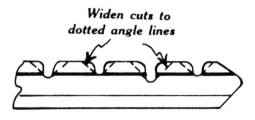

Widen cuts to dotted angle lines

Figure 74

The next tough point is to stop when you don't see a mark anymore. Now the key may not have impres-

sioned well, and the pin stack is not really at shearline yet, but you don't know that, so immediately stop when no more marks are seen. If you get all done (no marks at all) and the key still will not fit the lock, make a little harder impression and look very closely for marks, and one or two may become visible. If you are having trouble seeing the marks, it may be advisable to polish to the depth of a sixteenth of an inch or more. It will become necessary to provide angles leading down into the key cut bottoms. See Figure 74.

If these are not provided, the pins will catch at the cut bottoms and the key is forever frozen in the lock, requiring dissassembly. The angles should be 45 degrees or more — examine a couple of house keys and duplicate that angle. The actual cutting can be done with a small triangular mill file. Be very careful not to increase the cut depth, though.

Okay, let's assume you just impressioned the key and the lock opened. Touch up and straighten any crooked cuts in the key (but don't alter cut depths), and polish the entire keyblade with emery cloth, especially if guide lines are scribed on the key. Now, as a precaution, blow the keyway out with air to prevent key filings or chips from getting in the pin wells.

Now, let's suppose that you cut too deep — what next? Well, never fear. The easy way to build back the key surface is to rap the side of the blank carefully with a "ball," as in ball-peen hammer. This will flatten the metal (you did hit it on the side, didn't you?) and effectively make the cut shallower. If the damage cannot be repaired by this method, you must start over.

The final word on impressioning is practice, practice, practice. This skill requires good mark reading ability, but it is the opening skill that most locksmiths use to effect a lock-out or keyless entry, because when completed, the customer has a key that will work. It is also the preferred method of truly professional lock specialists, because once the opening is effected, it can be duplicated in a fraction of the time for subsequent visits. Also, the lock may be impressioned with a rest period between sessions, impossible with other lock bypass techniques, because of the necessity of keeping tension on the lock core.

Just briefly, there is another impressioning system out in which the key is turned as usual, but then pulled out of the lock about a sixteenth of an inch with great force and slowly (special tool needed for this). This system is not superior, but is easier on the lock. Although disc tumbler locks can be impressioned successfully with up and down impressioning, the pull system will not damage these locks, where up and down usually does. A resourceful person could probably improvise a slammer from a length of rod with a threaded end with two lock nuts on it, a large weight like a roll of washers taped together, and a hook to fit in the keyblank on the other end, but I have not experimented with this idea fully. I prefer the up and down system because of the ease of mark reading. A final caution: use a soft faced hammer when tapping the keyblank or the bow may suffer a lot of damage.

Chapter Twenty Four
Miscellaneous Other Tools

The Snapper

Another tool that is very useful is the snapper. For this tool from one-sixteenth inch o.d. music wire 18 inches long, start bending with the hook end and proceed back. See Figures 75 and 76.

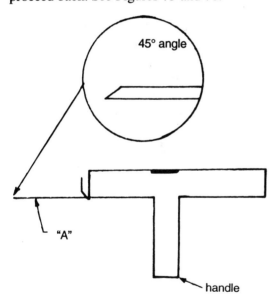

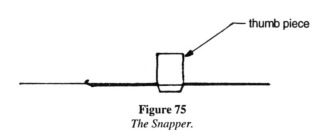

Figure 75
The Snapper.

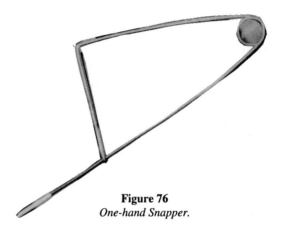

Figure 76
One-hand Snapper.

When you get to the "A" end, hook it in and cut it so that there is 1½ inches sticking past the loop. Grind flats as before on the sides of the wire so that it will fit in under the pins like a pick does. Be sure to grind at least one inch of the rod. Then grind a 45° taper on the end to enable it to slip under the pin ends. You may also want to taper the handle and the thumbpiece. This tool is a vibration pick. The ground end is inserted to contact the bottoms of all of the pins in the lock. Then a tension tool is inserted in the keyway. Hold the tool by the handle and push down the thumbpiece, then suddenly release, allowing the loop to hit the shank, transmitting vibration to the pins via the shank. By varying the tempo of snapping, and the level of tension exerted, a point will come when all of the top pins in the lock will be in the air. At this point, the lock plug will suddenly turn. A good operator can often open a lock with one snap.

A Tool For
Opening Office Equipment

A tool useful for opening office equipment locks can be made merely by bending a .030″ music wire in a "J" shape as shown in Figure 77.

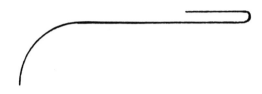

Figure 77
"J" Tool

Wrap tape around the loop to form a handle. This tool is inserted in the bottom of the keyway, ending with the "J" end pointing down at the rear of the lock. On many locks this end will engage the same slot that the cam on the tail of the lock plug engages. Then you can twist the handle and bypass the lock entirely. Manufacturers lately have wised up, though, and put a blocking pin in to prevent this. Even then, this technique is sometimes still useable — and for older equipment, it's great!

Tools For Spring Latches

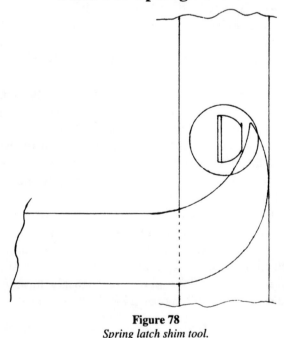

Figure 78
Spring latch shim tool.

Now let's take a look at the tools that act on the spring latch common on most exterior and interior lock sets. This is the wedge-shaped latch that locks automatically, not the bolt that must be locked by key. Those latches that are exposed, i.e., the latch can be seen, are a snap to open. A half-moon shim cut from one-sixteenth inch thick stock as shown in Figure 78, can be inserted behind the latch and levered against the bevel to open.

Tools For The Dead-Locking Latch

A dead-locking latch, consisting of an extra bar of metal parallel to the latch that does not enter the latch strike, but instead blocks on the strike plate, will prevent you from doing the half-moon bit, but I have seen doors fit so loosely that by forcing the door more tightly closed, the dead-locking bar suddenly snaps into the strike pocket. This releases the dead-lock and the latch can then be shimmed as usual. If the latch is not exposed (is covered by the stop), then you know it bevels the opposite way. The traditional plastic strip or credit card works fine, unless the traditional homeowner has installed nails, plates, cut a saw slot, or otherwise made it impossible for the card end to round the corner. In cases like this, the "Z" wire can save the day. As Figure 79 shows, the "Z" wire is only a .060″ or one-sixteenth inch o.d. music wire with two right angle bends, inserted and pivoted as shown.

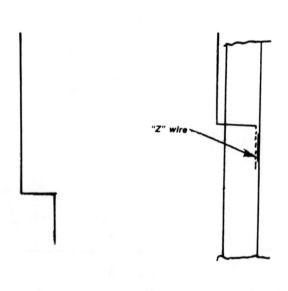

Figure 79
"Z" wire and "Z" wire engaging latch.

You will probably have to push on the door to gain clearance for inserting, and pull on the doorknob while working the tool. If a dead-locking latch is encountered in the non-exposed latch, attack the lock with your professional lock tool and forget the latch, because it won't budge.

Recommended Reading

The Complete Metalsmith by Tim McCreight. Davis Publications, 1991. This book is oriented to jewelers, but it is very good. Cuttlebone casting techniques are described which can be used to duplicate keys in metal.

Jewelry Concepts & Technology by Oppi Untracht. Doubleday, 1982. This book cost $100, but is worth every penny. It covers every conceivable area of metalworking. With this book and mine at your disposal, you'll be pickin' on top of the world.

Machinist's Bedside Reader by Guy Lataurd, 2570 Roseberry Avenue, West Vancouver, BC, Canada V7V 2Z9. Free, if you send this fellow a SASE, keep in mind that Canada requires more postage than the USA. This book is good for general machinists' tricks and tips, but offers nothing specific regarding lock picks per se.

WoodMet Services, Inc., 3314 West Shoff Circle, Peoria, IL 61604. These guys publish plan sets for wood- and metalworking stuff from scratch. Some smarts are required for comprehension, but they provide good information not available anywhere else.

Eddie gets no money from any of these gazooties. They are simply the best material on his shelf.

YOU WILL ALSO WANT TO READ: